POTOMAC JOURNEY

Fairfax Stone to Tidewater

Smithsonian Institution Press

Washington and London

POTOMAC JOURNEY

Richard L. Stanton

Editors: Robin A. Gould and William Charles Bennett, Jr.
Production Editor: Rebecca Browning
Designer: Janice Wheeler

Library of Congress Cataloging-in-Publication Data
Stanton, Richard L.
Potomac journey : Fairfax Stone to tidewater / Richard L. Stanton.
    p.   cm.
Includes bibliographical references.
ISBN 1-56098-218-7
1. Potomac River Valley—History. 2. Potomac River—History. I. Title.
F187.P8S73   1993
975.2—dc20   92-35179

British Library Cataloguing-in-Publication Data available
Manufactured in the United States of America

02 01 00 99 98 97 96 95 94 93
10 9   8   7   6   5   4   3   2   1

The paper used in this publication meets the minimum requirements of the American National Standard for Permanance of Paper for Printed Library Materials Z39.48-1984.

For permission to reproduce illustrations appearing in this book, please correspond directly with the owners of the works, as listed in the individual captions.

The photograph on the front cover is by Richard L. Stanton. On the back cover, the aerial view of Heaters Island (*top*) is courtesy of the National Park Service; the photograph of the *Minnie Lee* (*middle*) is by Kenneth Garrett; and the picture of the canal boat leaving a lock (*bottom*) is from the Helmer Collection. On the back flap is a snapshot of the author by John G. Parsons.

The epigraph, "Following a Star," a poem in free-form verse, was written by Linda Toms for this book.

To Sarah Jane

following a star
        most have never seen
the river offers refuge
    escape
        freedom—
            for the imprisoned spirit

        Tiâ

CONTENTS

Foreword

**A river is more than an amenity, it is a treasure . . . Mr. Justice
Holmes, Delaware River Opinion, 1931**

In the long span of years after the first European settlements were
established in North America, the rivers of this vast continent did
not need stewards. As a mighty force of nature, rivers were as unruly
as oceans and they evoked a respect bordering on awe in the people
who lived on their banks, harvested their fish, or sought to use them
as "highways" for travel. Rivers were wondrous places to the Canadian trappers who called themselves *voyageurs,* to the men who
struggled upriver with Lewis and Clark, and to Henry David
Thoreau as he maneuvered his canoe along some of New England's
unsullied streams.

But the Industrial Revolution and the advent of modern engineering changed the outlook of Americans toward their rivers. Demon-
strations that water could be harnessed to provide a source of energy
for textile mills turned some eastern rivers into sluiceways. The con-
cept that factories should be located along rivers and use their waters
to dilute their effluents converted many into industrial sewers. And
the discovery that the energy of falling water could be harnessed to
generate electricity produced a scramble by utility companies to acquire rights to develop the hydropower potential of rivers by building dams that turned free-flowing streams into man-made lakes.

For many decades, the Potomac River was shielded from the impacts of these and other modernizing trends. Even though Senator George Norris, one of the influential advocates of hydropower, bemoaned the "waste" of energy he had witnessed at Great Falls, no dam was built on the main stem of the Potomac during the river-harnessing frenzy of the New Deal era. The rich history of this stream (a history that included George Washington's effort to build a Potowmack Canal along its banks) provided some protection—and development was also slowed by an upland watershed that encompassed a rugged hinterland.

What adds fascination to Dick Stanton's story of the conservation of the resources of this river is that his stewardship began in the 1950s just as engineers arrived on the scene with grandiose plans to alter the environment of the Potomac Valley. Highwaymen unveiled a plan to build a freeway up the Maryland side of the river that would have altered the ambiance of the Potomac and obliterated the historic structures and quiet byways of the C & O Canal. And the Army Corps of Engineers presented a scheme for the "comprehensive development" of the Potomac Basin featuring assorted dams to protect the inhabitants from floods and to provide water for the growing Washington metroplex.

My appreciation of the author's account of the conservation battles that ensued has two dimensions. Like Dick Stanton, I had a personal love affair with the Potomac. Our home in McLean, Virginia, overlooked the river, and it provided sights and sounds and opportunities for outdoor recreation that enveloped our lives. I taught my children to fish at Little Falls. We canoed in the riffles below Great Falls. We shared the excitement of the shad runs, and witnessed the drama of the big floods, which, each spring, refreshed the resources of this undammed river.

In the 1960s by order of the President of the United States, I became deeply involved for two years in the preparation of a total environmental plan—the first for any U.S. river—to make the Potomac a "model of beauty and recreation for the entire country." This plan set high environmental goals, and Stanton provides many insights concerning the impact this planning process had on the politics of conservation in the Potomac Basin.

Potomac Journey is an inspiring book. More than any living individual I know, Dick Stanton deserves the appellation Riverkeeper of the Potomac. We are fortunate to have him, with his knack for telling river stories, guide us downriver over the same rocks and eddies navigated by George Washington's boatmen over 200 years ago.

Stewart L. Udall

Santa Fe, New Mexico

January 1993

Preface

The Potomac's edge is beautiful with its abundance of silver maples and majestic sycamores . . . we cannot get enough of them. The game fish are back, both above and below Washington. There are few rivers in this nation that are so ideally suited for small-boat exploration and adventure above their tidewater falls.

The Potomac is two rivers. The lower one is the broad and stately river of Captain John Smith, Mount Vernon, the great freight schooners, and tidewater settlements. It flows some 101 miles from Washington to its mouth, 11 miles wide where it enters the Chesapeake Bay.

The upper Potomac above Washington is the one I like best. It is the river of Thomas Cresap, Indian raids, the Potomac Company, and the Chesapeake and Ohio Canal. From its boisterous beginnings at the Fairfax Stone in Grant County, West Virginia, it plunges 281 miles to meet tidewater at the District of Columbia line. Yes, the upper Potomac is my river. It represents a lifetime of discovery for me and the rewards have been boundless.

The Potomac is characterized as the Nation's River and indeed it is. Gone are the days of irreversible pollution and massive fish kills. Little by little the Potomac's waters are becoming cleaner as treatment plants continue to be placed on line. Healing continues and the concerned citizen has replaced the disinterested bureaucrat. Continuing efforts to clean up the Potomac and cherish it are paying off, but there is always more to do.

Summer was always my favorite time of year. School was out and I was free to roam. My beat was the West End and Georgetown along the river, near where I lived. My summer uniform was a shirt, shorts, and a pair of floppy Keds. I hung around the canoe clubs and I would beg canoe rides to Three Sisters Island or as far downstream as Mason's (Roosevelt) Island and back. Those were peaceful days. The dreaded floods of 1936 were still a couple of years away.

A young boy named Tony was my constant companion. He lived with his brother in a summer shack wedged above Key Bridge and downstream of the Virginia Palisades. There was a large canoeing colony above Key Bridge and significant remnants still exist today on the District of Columbia side of the Potomac. There was a constant shunting of canoes back and forth from Georgetown to the Virginia side of the river. Canoes competed with massive gravel barges towed by coal-fired tugboats, churning back and forth as they worked the Marcey Creek ravine below Little Falls.

I have personal journals covering every canoe trip I have taken in my lifetime. They start in the summer of 1936; to date, I have documented 9,208 miles by canoe paddle, pole, and portage. Most of those miles have taken place on the Potomac River and its tributaries.

To know the Potomac you must drink it, swim in it, tremble as lightning strikes it, feel its icy cold, fight against its currents, and all but drown in it. You must feel its pulse through the bottom of a boat, be able to estimate the river's speed, understand its telling rock formations, and contemplate the great forces that have caused so many changes in the Potomac over the millennia. I have experienced all these things and you will find my passions reflected in the portions of my journals that follow.

Richard L. Stanton
Hagerstown, Maryland
Summer 1992

Acknowledgments

Rousing cheers and thanks are in order for my fellow members of Washington's Canoe Cruisers Association who, over the years, explored every corner of the Potomac and its tributaries with me. I also thank my many friends in the Potomac Valley who taught me to savor the notable events of the historic Chesapeake and Ohio Canal.

A debt of gratitude is due Robin A. Gould and Charles Bennett who patiently and skillfully edited my original manuscript and for Robin's helpful advice in the production of this volume.

Finally, I wish to thank Peter Cannell, Science Acquisitions Editor for the Smithsonian Press, who first encouraged me to undertake writing this book and never lost faith that the project would eventually succeed.

I also dedicate this book to the 8,700 volunteers who so unselfishly devoted an entire year removing flood debris and cleaning up the C & O Canal Park after the disastrous flood of 1985.

All of you have enriched my life beyond measure.

POTOMAC JOURNEY

Chapter 1.

HARD ROCKS AND SOFT

Starting as a brawling mountain stream, narrow enough to jump across, the Potomac River begins a long journey from the Fairfax Stone, near Kempton, Maryland, at an elevation of 3,140 feet above sea level. The 382-mile river flows swiftly to the southeast, exposing varying rock strata along the way. The Potomac Basin drains 14,670 square miles. Its river flows through six physiographic provinces, each with its own distinctive characteristics. It races through high mountains, ridges, fertile valleys, lowlands, and eventually across the soft sediments of the Coastal Plain. As it moves eastward, it becomes ever-widening until, at the river's 11-mile-wide mouth, it mixes with the waters of the Chesapeake Bay, where its long journey comes to an end.

The Allegheny Plateau, through which the North Branch of the Potomac flows, is the westernmost geologic slice of the Potomac River Basin. This province spans the land from the top of the Allegheny Mountains easterly to the Allegheny Front, just west of Cumberland, Maryland. The Allegheny Plateau is also referred to as the Appalachian Plateau. It is an area of narrow valleys and steep ridges, some reaching elevations of over 3,000 feet. Steep slopes make streams flow swiftly, and low soil permeability causes frequent

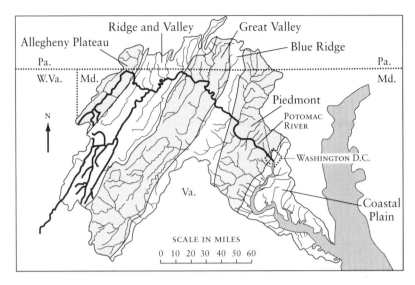

The Potomac River Basin drains 14,640 square miles and crosses six physiographic regions.

landslides. This part of the basin lies southeast of Deep Creek Lake and is characterized by horizontally bedded sedimentary rocks, mostly sandstone, shale, and limestone. Great quantities of coal are still found in the Allegheny Plateau. It is estimated that some 200 million tons of medium- to high-grade coal in seams 27 inches and over remain in this highest province of the Potomac Basin. Much of it is Upper Freeport, a metallurgical coal. This coal can lie hundreds of feet below the surface. Deep mining has started again along the crest of Backbone Mountain at Table Rock in Garrett County.

The Ridge and Valley province, home to the Potomac's South Branch and the Great Valley, constitutes about 60 percent of the Potomac Basin. This area is similar to the Allegheny Plateau, but is more intensely folded and faulted and is made up of older rocks. Also it lacks marketable coal. The Ridge and Valley province is made up of a series of parallel valleys separated by long, steep ridges. The Great Valley is located in the easternmost section. The softer shales have eroded to form the narrow but fertile valleys that rise in elevations of 500 to 1,000 feet. This is a province of thin, erodible soils.

The Great Valley in Maryland is sometimes called the Appalachian

Sideling Hill highway cut. (Courtesy John Thrasher)

Following Route 522 across the Potomac for a few miles brings you to Berkeley Springs, West Virginia. A sharp right turn in the center of town puts you on Route 9 (west) and, within a few minutes, you arrive at a scenic overlook above the town of Great Cacapon, called Prospect Peak. Five-hundred feet below the overlook, the Potomac turns northeast on its final rolling 7-mile journey to Hancock. Ahead and to the west you can also see the solitary Sideling Hill, 4 miles distant. The river has patiently scoured a wide, spectacular passage through Sideling Hill to the river's level of 500 feet. The passage is about $2\frac{1}{4}$-miles wide including the river and the land areas and hill slopes on either side of the Potomac.

The Paw Paw Bends lie in a broad valley farther west, with Sideling Hill bordering on the east and Town Hill on the west. Sideling Hill is a syncline, the bottom of a folded strata rather than the top of a fold. The crest is capped with purslane sandstone, a sandstone and quartz conglomerate extremely resistant to erosion.

Sideling Hill "sidles," meaning it leans to one side. This description can be traced back to the early eighteenth century. Town Hill, nearby, is similar in geological structure to Sideling Hill. Most other ridges in the area are anticlines, which are higher in the middle than at the ends; thus, anticlines are roughly parallel to the contours of the mountains.

There is much to learn by studying the gap at the old river cut, caused by the Potomac's unrelenting scouring. A clean, exposed cut would do nicely here and, as if by magic, the public now has a rare and unique opportunity to see a fresh exposed cut where Sideling Hill crosses Maryland Route 48, just inside the Maryland state line, only 6 miles northeast of the old cut.

The Route 48 cut is located just 6 miles west of Hancock, Maryland, in Washington County. This highway road, cut through Sideling Hill, exposes 850 feet of strata in a tightly folded syncline. The elevation of this cut is 100 feet lower than the primitive natural river cut to the south. This massive cut sliced a clean wedge out of Sideling, at a steep angle, and removed enough debris and rocks to allow a close view of sedimentary rock types, structural features, and geomorphic relationships. The tightly folded syncline seen here resulted from the enormous compressional stresses developed in the earth's crust by the collision of the North American and African continents in the late Permian or early Triassic period, 240 million years ago.

Valley, and it becomes the Shenandoah Valley south of the Potomac in Virginia. It is one of the most important agricultural areas in the eastern United States. It is part of a northeast-trending corridor ranging from 15 to 26 miles wide that runs from Alabama to Pennsylvania. It is largely underlain by easily erodible shales and more common carbonate rocks, primarily limestone and dolomite, which are folded and faulted. The dominance of solution openings in the carbonate rocks has made the valley an aquifer. Massanutten Mountain is the only enfolded evidence of the younger, more resistant sandstones that rise upward from the valley floor in excess of 2,000 feet.

The Blue Ridge province commonly rises and crests at 1,500 to 4,000 feet. The highest point is Hawksbill Mountain at 4,049 feet along the Shenandoah Parkway, 45 miles below Front Royal. This province forms a narrow boundary of rock 8 to 10 miles wide. All stream-flow from west of the Blue Ridge Mountains flows through the Harpers Ferry Gap.

From a scenic overlook near Great Cacapon, West Virginia, one follows the Potomac River west 4 miles where the river has, over a period of some 30 million years, scoured a natural passage through Sideling Hill (in background). The natural cut is about 2¼ miles wide including the river and land areas on either side of the Potomac. (Photo by M. Woodbridge Williams, courtesy of the National Park Service)

From its origins in the Allegheny province, the Potomac enters the Piedmont, passing through the lowland in the highly erodible Leesburg Basin and Frederick Valley. The rolling and hilly terrain of the Piedmont proper overlies hard and resistant crystalline rocks.

The Potomac, in the 33 miles between Point of Rocks to Great Falls, 10 miles above Washington, is a typical piedmont river, flowing through a valley bound in places by high, rocky palisades. In its ravines one finds multicolored spring flowers that flourish in the rock crevasses: gold moss; ditch stonecrop with its inconspicuous yellow-ish green flowers; false Solomon's seal, its fruit a translucent ruby red; wild leek and wake robin. In the Piedmont's soil are found beauties such as hepatica; golden ragwort, with yellow daisy-like flower heads in flat-topped clusters; jack-in-the-pulpit, the Indian turnip; bloodroot, a solitary white flower with a golden orange center; Dutchman's breeches, resembling tiny white pantaloons; wild ginger; columbine, seeker of perpendicular rock cliffs sheltered and sunny, showy and drooping, with bell-like flowers; and cranesbill, a wild geranium in delicate hues of rose, pale purplish blue, and white.

Erosion is always a problem throughout the Appalachian basin, a result of the combination of erodible soils with long-term urbanization, agricultural land use, and rainfall.

The Coastal Plain is reached just below Little Falls at Chain Bridge, the "fall line," where the Potomac takes a series of plunges that begin at Great Falls, dropping about 100 feet before reaching Chain Bridge. Soils from there on are naturally poor and excessively drained. From there the river comes under tidal influence and finally expands into a broad estuary as it enters Chesapeake Bay.

The Potomac River is said to have been in existence since the Miocene epoch, 30 million years ago. During the life of the river, the Potomac and its tributaries have carved out the Appalachian Mountains in this region as we see them today.

Chapter 2.

RUNNING THE RIVER

At Fairfax Stone, at the foot of Backbone Mountain, you are at the top of the world of the Potomac, 3,140 feet above sea level and virtually straddling the Potomac and Ohio watersheds. A hypothetical bucket of water poured on Backbone's crest would be divided and flow half to the east to the Atlantic Ocean and half to the northwest to join the Ohio and the Mississippi. Here is where the Potomac and the Ohio watersheds meet, at the edge of the Beaver Creek area, near Thomas, West Virginia, in one of the most rugged and beautiful parts of West Virginia and western Maryland.

If you follow the river through the Allegheny Plateau on its downward plunge from Kempton, Maryland, you will pass through the most spectacular and inaccessible mountains in the East. To the northwest, Backbone Mountain rises to reach the highest elevation in Maryland (3,360 feet above sea level). To the northeast, the Allegheny Front reaches elevations up to 3,000 feet to dominate the thin and wavy line of the Potomac's North Branch, barely seen threading its way within the river's trenches far below. The river rushes downward in torrents, finally reaching level land at the Savage River confluence, 46 precipitous miles downstream. In these 46 miles, the North Branch drops 2,000 feet, 43 feet per mile.

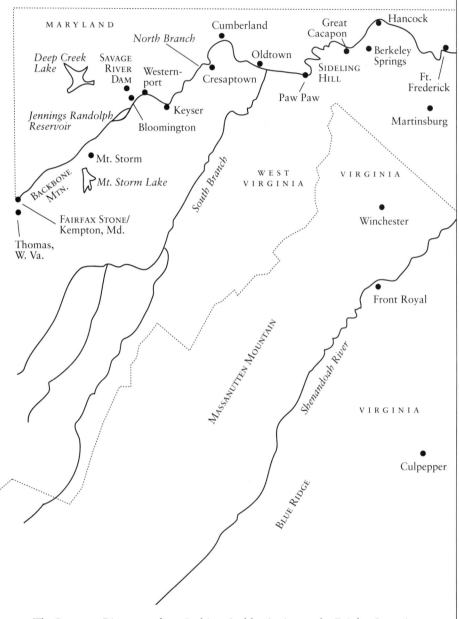

The Potomac River runs from its historical beginning at the Fairfax Stone in Grant County, West Virginia, at an elevation of 3,140 feet above sea level, 382 miles to its mouth at Point Lookout, Maryland, where it empties into the Chesapeake Bay.

PENNSYLVANIA

MARYLAND

Monocacy River

● Williamsport

● Sharpsburg
● ANTIETAM
  BATTLEFIELD
● ● Buckeystown

Shepherdstown

Baltimore

Harpers
Ferry

● Point of Rocks

● Whites Ferry

Seneca ●

● Rockville

Annapolis ●

Great Falls ●

VIRGINIA

● *Little*
Vienna *Falls*

Washington D.C.

● Fairfax

● Alexandria

Chesapeake Bay

● Manassas

MASON NECK

Warrenton ●

● Indian Head

Patuxent River

● Fredericksburg

St. Mary's
City ●

SCALE IN MILES

0   5   10   15   20   25

N

Point
Lookout

The river is one continuous rapid for 46 harrowing miles with little letup. I have refrained from boating these tortuous miles, preferring instead to explore the deep folds of these mountains by foot, along roads, paths, and railroad rights-of-way. You can become hopelessly lost in these hills, and even a minor boating accident can cost you your life. People, houses, and landscapes seldom change up here, yet there is something magical about this country with its deep green forested slopes, abandoned strip mines, and picturesque remains of yesterday's coal mining communities.

This part of the basin is distinguished by horizontally bedded sedimentary rocks, mostly shale, and some limestone. Coal has been mined here for well over 150 years. Mine acid drainage from abandoned mines has rendered half of the North Branch and more than 700 miles of its tributaries totally devoid of aquatic life. Groundwater is usually very hard. Deer are seen in abundance everywhere and the herds continue to increase.

The North Branch of the Potomac is a typical Appalachian river that, long ago, was turned over to heavy industry and coal mining. The land has been abused, scarred, and poisoned by acid mine drainage and, here and there, befouled by a familiar paper mill stench. Ten miles above the mouth of the Savage River, the North Branch opens up for 7 miles to accommodate Jennings Randolph Reservoir, which, it is hoped, will become the long-term salvation of the North Branch by diluting mine acid wastes. It will be necessary to reclaim many of the abandoned mines to make the North Branch of the Potomac River whole again, but so far, this appears to be a slow and almost hopeless task.

I have boated the North Branch from Keyser, West Virginia, stumbling, by open canoe, into the lethal spout in high water at the top of the Celanese Dam above Cumberland, then through milky trash-laden water in a long-dead pool that ends at a 15-foot waterfall, where Ridgely, West Virginia, meets Cumberland, Maryland. Unless you are a diehard whitewater enthusiast, willing to exhaust yourself along the miles and miles of continuous North Branch wildwater, I urge that all your through-trips begin just below Cumberland at the Potomac Edison substation across from Ridgely, West Virginia. I

Dick Stanton paddles solo just below Paw Paw, West Virginia. (Photo by John G. Parsons)

have three through-trips under my belt from Cumberland to Washington, each 197 miles long, and that is where I began all three.

One solo trip occurred from June 3 to 15, 1984. The purpose of the trip was to experiment and contemplate what it must have been like for Potomac River boatmen to run the full length of the river from Cumberland to the Georgetown wharves in the eighteenth and early nineteenth centuries. During the Potomac Company days, there was a natural dam just below the confluence of the Potomac and Wills Creek called Cumberland Falls. Years before, it had been known as Hoyes Dam, named after John Hoye, one of the founders of the city of Cumberland. Boatmen, their longboats, and cargoes would frequently capsize on the crest of this impediment. The exasperated boatmen would plant tall poles in the river to mark danger points, but still the boatmen would lose cargoes. Eventually, the natural dam was removed to make way for the C & O's Dam No. 8 in 1850.

The middle of May and first week in June are the best times to float the river up here. Usually, the heavy rains have abated and it is deliciously cool during the day. Late spring and early summer wildflowers are found along the river banks and the birds that follow the river are noisy and flashy.

Below the confluence of the North Branch and Wills Creek, a different Potomac appears. The air now seems pure, and flocks of fish crows join in the celebration with their distinctive calls—their goal, to hunt the nearest unwary owl, pin it down, and drive it to distraction. Now and then fish break the surface of the water ahead for a quick fish-eye view of the world above them.

As I pass down the North Branch, I see no life in the water or along the river banks, or even birds winging above the surface of the river. Five miles above Cumberland rise the highest and most dramatic palisades to be found anywhere along the Potomac and its tributaries. The Knobly Mountain Palisades, across the river from the Cumberland Fair Grounds, rise to elevations of 1,500 feet, 900 feet above the river.

Canoe and equipment must be carried around a 15-foot dam at Cumberland. After moving to the mainstem Potomac, matters change and the patches of woods along the margins of the river are alive with deer, bank muskrat, squirrel, skunk, and beaver. I know where the wild turkeys are. I have seen them in the same places over and over. They like open terrain, that's why they seek the C & O Canal towpath, sometimes walking in platoons of 20 to 30 at a time. They will let you get near and act as though they don't even know you're around, then, as if by signal, they speed up and manage, again, to stay far enough ahead where they are safe. When they become uneasy, the entire flock will take off quickly, then settle down when it feels all is well. They really prefer not to fly.

Trains join in now and will follow the river route to Georgetown for miles. The heavy roar of the engines boom and their shrill whistles make a happy sound.

High on a hill, in back of me, under Emmanuel Church, lie the underground remains of parts of Fort Cumberland, originally a trading post used by the Indians and the British when fur trading flourished here. The interior of the church is warmed by a grand Tiffany stained-glass window, which floods the church with joy and beauty. Wills Creek and a nearby mountain were both named after Indian Will, an early Cumberland settler. Thomas Cresap, famous Indian

Confluence of the South Branch with the North Branch (upper left) of the Potomac River. (Photo by M. Woodbridge Williams, courtesy of the National Park Service)

trader and frontiersman, was also an early settler. Cresap, with Indian guide Nemacolin, built the first road to the West through the wilderness from Fort Cumberland to the tributary waters of the Ohio near Fort Duquesne (Pittsburgh). Both General Braddock and George Washington used this path during the French and Indian War. It later became known as Braddock's Road, winding through the Allegheny Mountains.

Next, I laboriously carry boat and equipment around a rock dam a mile above the sparse community of North Branch, one of several carries along the 197-mile through-route to Georgetown. Greenspring Road crosses the canal and the river at Oldtown, over a low toll bridge where, on the West Virginia side, track ties are creosoted, then stacked to the sky.

The temperamental North Branch of the Potomac flows generally northeast until it meets the mouth of the South Branch, east of

Cumberland. It is at the confluence of the South and North branches, below Oldtown, where the Potomac River sheds its two branches and proceeds on its own. The Potomac graduates into a full-fledged river at this precise point, although few river travelers are aware of the change. In addition, with the flow of the South Branch now behind it, the Potomac River widens and quickens and will stay that way for most of its journey downstream.

On the left, just past the South Branch confluence, lies the extensive sweep once known as King Opessa's town, where King Opessa's Shawnee warriors flourished, providing plenty of room for tribesmen who roamed up and down the South Branch valley. Later, in 1742, Thomas Cresap made his home here at Oldtown, then referred to as Shawnee Old Town. Cresap built a stockade fort and called it Fort Skipton from which he traded furs with passing Indians. Skipton was the name of Cresap's birthplace in England. He was born about 1703 and died in 1790, near the age of 87. Passing visitors included George Washington, General Braddock, and many pioneers on their way to settle the West. Until a shorter route was constructed, Cresap's fort was a stopping place for westbound stagecoach lines.

A side trip up the South Branch offers some of the most beautiful valley scenery anywhere. The mouth of the South Branch lies only 2 miles downriver from Oldtown. A 5-mile float through the Trough, just below Moorefield, West Virginia, will never be forgotten. Here, mountains rise 1,000 feet from the surface of the South Branch, creating a troughlike effect. George Washington described it as "Two Ledges of Mountain, impassable running side by side together for about 5 miles and ye river down between them." The 5-mile-long Trough offers an abundance of snakes, all manner of species. In the evenings, they begin their downward crawl to the edge of the river for water, rustling through dry leaves.

After sampling the South Branch, I re-enter the Potomac and head east to Paw Paw, West Virginia, where the 21-mile serpentine Bends begin, coursing through a wide valley. Aside from a narrow packed gravel road along the railroad tracks high above the river, the Bends lie in a virtually roadless area, which explains why the valley has remained relatively free from development. My first run through the Bends was in July 1957, some 35 years ago. Today, it is less devel-

Overlooking the Paw Paw Bends. (Photo by Richard Stanton)

oped than in earlier days, due to ruinous floods and the paucity of construction funds to build along riverside terraces that have little or no access.

The 3,118-foot Paw Paw Tunnel, which opened in 1850, allowed the C & O Canal to bypass 7 miles of difficult canal building. Some 6 million bricks were used in its construction. The tunnel and the surrounding countryside have changed little since the tunnel's completion in 1850. There is a huge eagle's nest high above the river just below Paw Paw, perched on the top of an abandoned railroad pier.

I continue through the broad Paw Paw Valley, surrounded by the high ridges of Sideling Hill, Green Ridge, Purslane Mountain, and Town Hill. Far ahead is an overlook, high above the river at the edge of Town Hill to the west. From this overlook, there is no finer panorama of the Paw Paw Valley and its river, flowing far below. I love this stretch of the river. I have documented over 100 visits through the Bends since July 1957.

Schonadel's store is located on the west side of the river, at Little Orleans, 22 river-miles below Paw Paw. Here is my last opportunity to satisfy hunger and thirst until Hancock, 17 more miles downriver.

After turning to the east at Turkey Foot Bend, I paddle at what was the bottom of a 5-mile pool. Historically, it was the backwater, held at a high level, behind feeder Dam No. 6. This is as far as the old C & O Canal Company reached in April 1839, having run out of money. Dam No. 6 was to become the head of navigation on the canal for over eight years. Coal from Cumberland was carried by rail to the (then) Virginia side of the river, off-loaded, and then transported to canal boats that proceeded down to Georgetown by entering the canal from a guard lock above Dam No. 6. Dam No. 6 has been reduced to rubble due to incessant damage from floods over the years. From the site of the old dam, I make an S-turn and travel right down the center of the rapids in the river. Dam No. 7 was never built. It was to have been constructed below the mouth of the South Branch.

I reach Hancock amidst traffic noise and confusion that doesn't let up for 10 miles. Fort Frederick, a state park, lies on the west side of the river, 13 miles below Hancock. In 1756, Provincial Governor Horatio Sharpe built Fort Frederick to protect Maryland against the French and Indians after General Braddock's ill-fated defeat along the Monongahela River in 1755. It is virtually impossible to locate from the river unless you keep on the lookout for wooden steps leading from the river to the fort.

Downriver, a mile and a half from Back Creek, lie the fiddle strings, so-called since the eighteenth century because, in low water, without the massive C & O Canal Dam No. 5 in place, there were four high ledges of rock near each other, extending across the river with only one passage for boats. The rock ridges looked like long fiddle strings. In medium to high water these rocks pose no problem.

C & O Canal Dam No. 5 is reached. I have now traveled 89 miles with only two carries behind me. Motorboats have been much in evidence for the past 10 miles. It is here at Dam No. 5 that the river scene begins to change once again. Summer cottages and boat docks take over, and the roll and pitch of the river, caused by the wakes of motorboats, make it difficult for smaller hand-propelled craft to manage. There is a new boating regulation that no craft is allowed to land less than 200 feet from the crest of Dams No. 4 and No. 5. In addition, class III PFDs (life jackets) must be worn from November

15 through May 15. The Maryland State Department of Natural Resources' police are serious about enforcing this regulation.

The river continues to Williamsport, where I am required to carry around the West Virginia side of the river above the Potomac Edison plant. The carry is well marked, but long and tedious. More summer cottages appear for several miles and at a bend in the river, the Potomac Fish and Game Club appears. I stop here a while. My fellow club members are always glad to say "Hello." They are a friendly lot and care very much about the river and the wildlife along its banks. Another club lies ahead, the Western Maryland Sportsman's Club, at Dam No. 4—a fine group of folks.

Another carry (my fourth), is at C & O Canal Dam No. 4. Some of the finest fishing on the upper Potomac can be found at the base of this dam on the downstream side. I would be foolhardy to try to see how close I could come to the bottom of Dam 4's falls, however. Presently, both Dam No. 4 and No. 5 have been found by the State of Maryland to be seriously undermined and are considered unsafe. Repairs are anticipated.

Now I am about to cover the 24 miles to Harpers Ferry from Dam No. 4, some of the most historic lands along the margins of the Potomac. After putting my boat in the river, which leaves Dam No. 4 behind at a furious pace, the river finally settles down to a safer and more comfortable speed. There are several limestone caves about a mile or more below Dam No. 4 on the towpath side of the river. We soon see the village of Mercersville, ahead, named after Charles Fenton Mercer, elected first president of the C & O Canal Company in 1828. Today, the village is known locally as Taylors Landing in memory of John Taylor who spent his life here. Below Taylors Landing, around a bend, I reach a wide part of the river called Cox's Widewater by the old canallers. Horseshoe Bend brings me to Snyders Landing, also known as Sharpsburg Landing during canal days. Sharpsburg lies only a mile from the river at this point and was much used by the old boatmen as a quick access to the village.

In low water, the remains of many fish traps can be seen along the river route to Harpers Ferry. This is limestone country, and we are moving through the heart of the Piedmont Valley (Great Valley) where many important Civil War events took place. There are more

Rare photograph of fish trap, circa 1913. (Courtesy of the National Park Service)

The remains of ancient and more contemporary fish traps are found in abundance along the Potomac. Many examples are also found in the Susquehannah, the James, the Delaware, and Schuylkill rivers.

The largest fish trap in the Potomac today is the massive trap just below Williamsport, running from shore to shore, a distance of one-eighth of a mile. One can see the trap in low water, looking up-stream from the U.S. Route 81 bridge.

Fish traps were constructed by placing medium- and large-sized stones one upon the other to a height of about 3-4 feet in the shape of a "v," with the apex of the "v" facing downstream. Fish were swept into the "v" and eventually wound up in the apex where they were forced into positions from which they could not escape. This was accomplished either through a buildup of brush at the apex from which the fish were extracted or through the use of a boxlike wood-en structure that allowed the fish to skid along the top at the apex then drop through slats into a waiting collection point below. The latter device is sometimes called a weir. Fish were so plentiful during colonial days they could be scooped out of the weir at the trap's apex end with ease or held for later collection with nets or brush enclosures.

Some of the remains of traps we see today may be Indian traps that have been repaired, built on, or relocated over the years. The colonial settlers took over whatever traps were still in the river by simply claiming possession. There is no doubt that a few of the sites we see today have been used for several hundred years or more, having been repaired over and over again. Water levels in the river run at differing speeds; the bottom layer of water makes the least progress. Because of this, the base layer of trap rocks seldom moves. Even after torrential floods, traps always reappear intact when water levels recede.

One problem with construction of the traps was the paucity of medium- and large-sized stones with which to build the structures. Some stones obviously had to be barged down from sites farther upriver. When the water is lower, I frequently point the bow of my canoe at the apex of an old fish trap, knowing that several inches of water will be there to help me glide through a shallow, barely scraping bottom. It works every time, but by no means were these traps used for boat navigation and they were not a part of the navigational works in the river during the Potomac Company heyday.

Fish traps and weirs became a hindrance to navigation on the river, especially during George Washington's Potomac Company era. Washington passed the word to have as many of the contraptions removed from the river as possible and frequently took legal action to deal with the traps.

"Captain" George Pointer, former slave, who had bought his freedom for $300, worked as a foreman on many of the Potomac Company jobs. He had been the keeper of the Little Falls Locks and a boatman before that. In a letter dated September 1789, Pointer relates that "inhabitants on the margin of the river had obstructed in great measure, the passage [of the river], both down and up by building fish potts" and that he was ordered by the company to "get hands, go up, and tear all down that in any manner tamed the water so as to obstruct the passage of boats." Pointer reported that of 73 pots, he and his crew took down 44.

One canaller I know recalled the trouble that brewed between fish-trap proprietors and sports fishermen in the 1930s. The trap proprietors refused to cooperate with Maryland by removing their traps and weirs so the state blew many of them out of the water with blasting powder, ending the fish trap era once and for all. Now they are illegal, but the bottom layers of the traps still lie stubbornly in place.

caves along this stretch of the river. One, it has been said, was used by the citizens of Sharpsburg for safety during the Battle of Antietam.

Above Shepherdstown are parallel limestone outcrops running with the river instead of across. These rocks are known as the "Horsebacks," and in medium water remind me of horses' backs about to rise from the surface of the water. In low water they are tricky to maneuver.

On the West Virginia side of the river I can see Shepherd College. A 75-foot-high ionic granite column rises above the Potomac, and commemorates James Rumsey and his successful steamboat trials that took place here in 1787. Rumsey was also chief engineer of the Potomac Company at Great Falls. On the north side of the river I can make out the remains of the Shepherdstown River lock where canal boats entered the canal from the river after loading at Boteler's hydraulic lime cement mill from the (then) Virginia side of the river. The mill furnished great quantities of cement used in building the C & O Canal. Less than a half-mile downstream, I pass over a shallow known as Packhorse Ford.

I stay on the right of the river, descending, and soon the river fetches to the right and I come upon Houses Falls, where a ledge of limestone crosses the river obliquely to feed Houses Falls sluice at the edge of the river, originally cut by John Semple before the Potomac Company received its charter. Later, it was used by the Potomac Company in its river freight hauling. Semple used the sluice to overcome 3 feet of ledges at Houses Falls to haul his Keep Tryst iron ore to the Antietam Iron Works, upstream.

From a distance I can make out the Harpers Ferry Gap from the center of the river, another thrilling panorama on the Potomac. I make my way through a rock-strewn labyrinth known as Shenandoah Falls (in the Potomac) by easing down the "needles" on the north side of the river. Once in the Gap, also called the Hole, the Blue Ridge is split and the Shenandoah adds its torrent of water at Paynes Falls located at the bottom of Shenandoah Falls. The mad rush to tidewater now begins. For many miles the river will be even wider and faster.

In the heart of Harpers Ferry Gap, Maryland Heights towers over the confluence of the Potomac and the Shenandoah rivers. On a flat

Harpers Ferry, circa 1916. (Courtesy of the National Park Service)

rock, about 240 feet above the river, are the faint remains of the Mennen's Borate Talcum Powder advertisement, painted, I am told, by a German immigrant in 1885. The painter used a mixture of goat's milk and whitewash. The advertisement was probably 15 feet high and 12 feet wide. The artist received the humble sum of $40 for his work. In the 1960s, the work was thought to be out of place so a group of well-meaning rockclimbers tried to erase the delightfully "camp" sign. Hanging from ropes with lamp-black erasers and permits in hand, the stalwarts began to erase the sign on the rock's face. We know now that today's generation, and indeed yesterday's, loved that sign. Thankfully, nature cooperated by shedding tears of rain and eventually returned what was left of the sign to a grateful public. It hasn't been touched since.

Leaving Harpers Ferry behind, I head east downriver, rushing across the Bull Ring, a dangerous upwelling. I am too committed to avoid the Spout (White Horse Rapid), and grip the boat with my

Georgetown waterfront below the University clock tower, circa 1915, virtually unchanged in the past 78 years. (Courtesy of the National Park Service)

knees and thighs, as I head into the chute. Weaverton Falls is next and then the straight run to Brunswick, 6 miles ahead. With the Shenandoah now behind me the river becomes wider. Next, I pass through the rapids at Point of Rocks. Heaters Island lies dead ahead and the water slows. I turn at the mouth of the Monocacy River to inspect one of the Canal Company's works of art, a seven-arch aqueduct that carried canal water, boats, cargoes, and crews up or down the canal. This magnificent structure is 516 feet long and was completed in 1833. Two varieties of quartzite, pink and white, were used in its construction, which were cut from the quarries located on the western slope of nearby Sugarloaf Mountain. The aqueduct has been strengthened with heavy steel straps and the cracks in the stone trunk and towpath sections have been sealed with heavy grouting to keep water from entering the masonry, thus protecting it from frost damage.

Next, I pass Whites Ferry, which has been in continuous operation for 150 years. At one time, there were over 100 ferries operating on the river. This is the last one. The current of the river is even slower now and will continue to run slowly until it reaches Seneca Falls. Across the river from Whites Ferry lies Harrison Island, known as Black Walnut Island many years ago. It is here, on the Virginia side of Harrison Island, that the Battle of Balls Bluff was fought in October of 1861, one of the earliest and bloodiest of Civil War battles. A national cemetery lies on a cliff above the river.

The river now widens until it reaches Seneca where the Seneca Bypass Canal was constructed by the Potomac Company. Most boaters take what is erroneously called "George Washington's Canal" on the far Virginia side of the river. Once in this labyrinth of channels, rocks, and trees, the passage becomes difficult. Above Great Falls I must make a decision on how the falls are to be overcome. Most boaters take out just above the Great Falls Tavern (the Crommelin House) on the Maryland side of the river and follow the canal to the base of Little Falls. Others carry to Anglers Inn (Cropley) 3 miles down the towpath and finish from there, making sure to avoid Little Falls. It can take boaters all day to cover the 11 miles to the base of Little Falls because of carries and towpath traffic.

The world changes at Little Falls. Fishermen crowd the river with rented rowboats. Ahead, the U.S. Capitol building and the Washington Monument can be seen in the distance. Traffic around the sites of the old canoe clubs, hugging the District of Columbia shoreline, is heavy, as usual. At times, long and slender rowing shells pierce the river, upstream or down, and refuse to move out of the way until the last moment. Georgetown lies to the north on a high promontory. The noise of the city is loud and annoying. I am soon floating past the stone steps of the Watergate, then under the classic lines of Memorial Bridge. The Lincoln Memorial stands nearby.

The river of the bass boat and canoe gives way to larger and more stable craft. As I proceed downriver, I notice the buildup of great blue heron, eagles, and osprey. There is an abundance of fish for the birds. I have seen more black-crowned night herons along the shores of the Potomac in the last few years than I have seen in my lifetime.

When a small craft drops down into the Potomac's waters at the base of Little Falls, it is said to have reached "tidewater." In some small measure it has, but the Potomac still has a long way to go before it reaches a noticeable salinity. In fact, salinity does not strength-

Point Lookout Lighthouse at the mouth of the Potomac River at the Chesapeake Bay, 382 miles from the historic source of the Potomac at Fairfax Stone. (Photo by Nicholas Dean)

en significantly until the river reaches Indian Head, Maryland. Parts of the stretch above Indian Head are sometimes called "the freshes." Below Indian Head, the river enters a mixing zone down to the Route 301 bridge across the river. From there, the Potomac mixes, in an increasing measure, with the salt waters of the Chesapeake Bay.

I still think about putting my frail canoe in Washington's waters to begin the complete 99-mile adventure from Georgetown to Point Lookout. I may do it someday, but so far I have not summoned the courage. I have reached the conclusion that tidewater is no place for small boats. I have sampled the river at points along the wide lower river by canoe and find that in any season and any weather, tidewater shores take continual pounding by wave action and unceasing rolling from boat wakes. Difficulties are further compounded by tides, and strong and capricious winds, sometimes with no let-up for days. Traversing from shore to shore would, at times, require a shuttle of 4 to 5 miles or more. And to think, at Kempton, I could have jumped across the Potomac!

Chapter 3.

EARLY AWAKENINGS

The first inhabitants of the Potomac River region were descendants of Asian immigrants who crossed the Bering Strait into Alaska over 14,000 years ago. By 10,000 B.C., these nomadic Paleoindians had reached the Potomac Valley, following migratory herds of now-extinct animals.

Sharp, fluted spear points found near Seneca, Point of Rocks, and recently in the Monocacy River Valley in Maryland, are among the artifacts along the Potomac that best represent the Paleoindian period. Similar spear points have been found near Front Royal, Virginia, and on the South Branch of the Shenandoah River. Ice sheets were still covering Canada during this period, and the climate in the Mid-Atlantic region, which includes the Potomac River Basin, was cool and dry. Hunters of this period preyed on large, now-extinct Pleistocene animals such as mammoths and mastodons, and no doubt exploited the waters of the Potomac.

With the retreat of the glaciers around 10,000 years ago, the climate warmed and oaks, chestnuts, and other deciduous trees began to replace conifers and grassland. The mammoth, the mastodon, and other big-game species died out, but were replaced with deer, bear, and animals we are familiar with today. Valley inhabitants relied on

Turtles basking in the sun. (Photo by Richard Stanton)

hunting as well as wild plant foods such as chestnuts and berries. Hunter-gatherer peoples of this Archaic period (8000–1000 B.C.) left notched and stemmed spear points, ground-stone axes, knives, pestles and grinding stones—examples of their methods of obtaining and processing food. The population was growing and, for the first time, artistry was combined with ceremonial activities. Occupation sites were simple, temporary camps. The cultural material from these sites suggests a marginal subsistence pattern by people who were dependent on game animals, vegetable products, and both fresh and salt water fish and shellfish.

Fired pottery marks the Woodland period (1000 B.C. to A.D. 1000). Low, conical or domed mounds were constructed for burials and the use of the bow and arrow characterize this period. Within the Potomac region, the mound-building culture is called the Adena. By A.D. 200 corn was being grown on the banks of the Potomac. Along with corn, beans, squash, and sunflowers became mainstay foods of the valley's Indians. Villages were large and mostly oval in pattern, and more often than not built close to the riverbank. Animal

Fish petroglyph, perhaps 1,300 years old, probably marking fishing area along river. Located downriver from Great Falls. (Photo by Richard Stanton)

bones excavated at a well-known archaeological site near Seneca indicate the diversity of animals that were sought for food and clothing: deer, squirrel, rabbit, beaver, skunk, racoon, fox, mink, bobcat, black bear, elk, turkey, duck, box turtle, snapping turtle, painted turtle, sturgeon, sucker, freshwater mussel, and river snails. A plentiful supply of game with a dependable agricultural base and an abundance of wild plants assured continuous good living in large measure for all manner of Indian occupants along the river during this period.

From A.D. 1000 to 1700 Indian cultures flourished, increasing their reliance on fish and shellfish. Many groups converged in spring on the Little Falls area when immense numbers of sturgeon, shad, and other species moved upriver to spawn. Captain John Smith, in his account of the discovery of the Potomac, wrote:

. . . in diverse places that abundance of fish lying so thicke with their heads above the water as for want of nets (our barge driving amongst them) we attempted to catch them with a frying pan, but we found it a bad instrument to catch fish with.

Archaeological sites representing all cultural periods have been discovered and examined: campsites, burial mounds and ossuaries, village sites, rock overhang sites, quarries, and fish traps. Reoccupation of the same sites over hundreds and thousands of years is the rule rather than the exception.

Prior to A.D. 1700, the Indians in the East organized themselves into confederacies. The Iroquois, sometimes known as Six Nations, were located to the north; the tribal lands of the Catawbas and Cherokees lay south of the James River. Between these extremes lay the Potomac region, where all Indians were known to trade and hunt and sometimes make war, but few permanent settlements were established. Some tribes considered this range of land sacred. Specific Indian groups and villages were occasionally recorded by early colonial settlers: Mayaone (Piscataway, an Algonquian group), Susquehannock (Susquehanna, an Iroquoian group), Nacotchtanks (Anacosin, an Algonquian group), and the Patawomeke (Potomac, an Algonquian group). These were located mostly on the lower Potomac River.

Early European visitors to the Potomac, especially the English, found the entire Potomac native population below Great Falls to be living in constant dread of the Susquehannocks, who had established themselves at the head of Chesapeake Bay. Weaker groups simply could not hold out against the destructive Susquehannock raiding parties and eventually relocated farther up the river.

The upper Piedmont and headwater areas on the Virginia side of the river were occupied mostly by Siouxan-speaking peoples. Subsequent population pressures and movement brought the Iroquoian-Susquehanna westward from the Chesapeake Bay region into the area on the Maryland side of the river. The Seneca, also Iroquoian, made periodic raids from the north into the Potomac River Valley as far down as the tidewater regions.

The upper Potomac River in the Maryland and West Virginia areas was mostly uninhabited, according to early colonial reports. The archaeological picture in the upper part of the Potomac Valley has

The Great Seal of the Patowmack
Company, 1803.

The word Potomac was shown on Captain John Smith's 1608 map
as Patawomeck after the Pawtomax Indians that lived near the confluence of what Smith called the Sherrendo (Shenandoah) and the
Cohaungoruton (Potomac) rivers. The popular translation of the
name Patawomeck is "they are coming by water." Additional tradi-
tional translations are "where goods are brought in" and "where
goods are traded." On early maps, the Potomac has a variety of
names: the Elisabeth River, Red River, and Maryland River. To early
Spanish travelers it was the Espiritu Santo, and in 1588, Captain
Vincente Gonzalez, sailing from St. Augustine (Florida), entered
the Bahía de Madre de Dios, the Bay of the Mother of God, now the
Chesapeake Bay, and at the approximate 38th degree of latitude,
"discovered" the mouth of the Potomac, and named it San Pedro.

To Lord Baltimore's pilgrims, the Potomac was the St. Gregory. The
late Charles Morrison, in his authoritative book *Wappatomaka*, lists
several Indian place names for the Potomac: *Pataromerke*, *Pata-
womecke*, *Pataomek*, *Patowmack*, and *Patomeck*. Will Lowdermilk in
his *History of Cumberland* notes that as far back as 1632, the year
of the grant to Lord Baltimore, the Potomac River from the mouth of
the Shenandoah to Wills Creek was also called *Ouiriough* by the
Shawnees, meaning "the place of the burning pine, resembling a
council fire."

Place names for the Potomac and its branches and tributaries abound. I've heard most of them and they are all beautiful. *Cohaungoruton,* the Wild Goose Stream, with its variable spellings, seems to be a popular historical name for the Potomac River above tidewater, excluding the Shenandoah and the two upper Potomac branches. The origin of the Indian place name for the South Branch is traceable to Captain John Smith's 1608 journey into Chesapeake Bay and is generally accepted as either *Wappatomaka* or *Wappacomo.*

Morrison also informs us that before Fort Cumberland was built, an Indian village existed on the same spot known as *Caiuctucuc,* meaning "where the gull river is" (the meeting of the waters of many fishes), which applied to nearby Wills Creek at Cumberland.

Shenandoah was certainly derived from *Shanadoa,* "river flowing alongside of hills." Then there is "daughter of the stars," which I like. Every Campfire Girl knows the Shenandoah by this name. Finally, the less well-known *Kahan-Galuta* is attributed to the North Branch of the Potomac River above its confluence with the South Branch, 2 miles below Oldtown, Maryland.

The Indian tribes in the valleys of the Potomac left no written history, so we have few reliable translations for Indian place names along the Potomac and its tributaries. The first European settlers and those who followed applied their own meaning to Indian language and culture. Both cultures have paid a high price for this lack of mutual understanding.

The 1803 Potomac Company seal was acquired by the United States in 1938 as part of the transfer of assets from the receivers of the Chesapeake and Ohio Canal Company. The spelling on the seal, Patowmack Company, is the last vestige of this era.

----

received only minor and superficial attention and surveys and excavations are still required. We know there was serious conflict among the tribes. Population pressures, brought on by the rapid European settlement and competition for the fur trade, caused deadly Indian infighting, leaving the Potomac piedmont almost uninhabited with the exception of hunting parties passing through.

Little by little, the Indians were driven out as the competition for game became fierce. Indians relocated, taking paths to western Pennsylvania and west to the Ohio territories, merging with other tribes of similar linguistic stock.

So, for over 10,000 years, Indian cultures were roaming the Potomac Valley, each group adding their shell heaps, projectile points, axe-heads, pottery sherds, human skeletons, and other objects, building rising carpets of artifacts and cultural evidence.

THE ARRIVAL OF EUROPEANS

Europeans came to the Potomac during the first half of the sixteenth century. The earliest explorer known to have sailed any considerable distance up the Potomac was the Spanish admiral, Pedro Menendez, founder of St. Augustine and governor of Spain's Florida possessions. In 1571, he ascended as far up as Occoquan Creek, 25 miles below what would become Washington, D.C. This voyage took place 36 years before Captain John Smith's exploration of the river's navigable head. Admiral Menendez's departure the same year marked the end of any Spanish influence in Potomac River history.

Although the Spanish were the first Europeans to explore the mouth of the Potomac in the second half of the sixteenth century, Captain John Smith is credited as the first European to discover the Potomac River in 1608, opening the Potomac River Basin to European exploration and settlement. Smith called it the "sweetest and greatest river" he had ever seen. Catholics and Protestants from England, followed by French Huguenots, quickly occupied the lands of the lower estuary and by the mid-seventeenth century began to move into the southern portion of the upper basin. From Pennsylvania and New York, Quakers and Germans migrated southward along the Shenandoah and Monocacy river valleys, establishing permanent communities along the way. In the mid-eighteenth century, the Scots-Irish took up lands in western Maryland and in what we now know as West Virginia.

On June 20, 1632, Charles I of England granted a charter to Cecelius Calvert, second Lord Baltimore, under the name "The Province of Maryland." The territory granted was bounded on the east by the Atlantic Ocean and the Delaware Bay and River; on the north by the 40th parallel of north latitude and on the west by a line drawn from the northern boundary southward to the most western source of the Potomac River, and then down the farther bank of that river to Cinquack, situated near the "mouth of said river where it disembogues into Chesapeake Bay"; then on the south by a line running from this last place to Watkins Point on the eastern shore of the bay, and then east to the Atlantic Ocean.

With the granting of the charter, all the land described was held by Lord Baltimore. It originally included the entire state of Delaware, a wide strip of the southern part of Pennsylvania, including Philadelphia, and a tract of land that belonged to the Commonwealth of Virginia. The charter boundaries were based on crude maps, prepared with little understanding of what the descriptions and lines meant. This marked the beginning of many years of boundary disputes.

Lord Baltimore was required under the charter to yield to the king, "two Indian Arrows of those Parts, to be delivered at the Castle of Windsor, every Year, on Tuesday in Easter-week: and also the fifth Part of all Gold and Silver Ore, which shall happen from Time to Time to be found within the aforesaid Limits." Lord Baltimore as the proprietor could make laws and appoint officers of the government with the consent of the freemen of the province. He could raise armies and go to war, hold courts of justice, and, in fact, enjoy all those rights and privileges of an independent king, but he could not levy taxes or in any way interfere with the liberties of the people within the province, in keeping with charter provisions.

Upon receipt of his charter, Lord Baltimore's first act was to send out a colony to settle the lands with his brother Leonard Calvert as governor. The first English colony would be established along the shores of the Potomac River. On board two ships, the 300-ton *Ark* and the 50-ton *Dove*, were twenty "gentlemen adventurers" and about two hundred colonists who sailed westward from England on November 22, 1633, prepared to conquer the vast unknown.

After a stormy passage, both vessels reached Point Comfort on the Virginia coast, then sailed up the Chesapeake Bay, entering the mouth of the Potomac River on March 25, 1634. After having endured a passage of four months, the soft shores of the Potomac beckoned with their fresh early springtime growth. Governor Calvert felt it essential to make friends as quickly as possible; along the shoreline

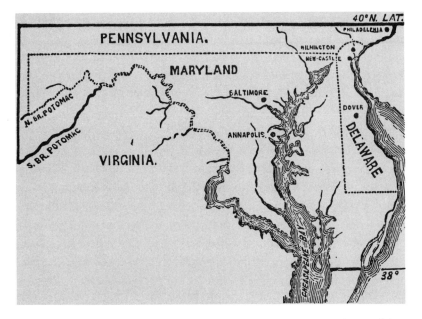

Initial land areas granted to Lord Baltimore. (The land north and east of the dashed line was eventually given to the Penns and the Duke of York by King Charles II.)

Indians could be seen tending their signal fires and their mood seemed hostile.

Armed Piscataway warriors were waiting, prepared to protect their emperor by any means. After many gestures of friendship and offerings by the colonists, peace was established. Governor Calvert and his "gentlemen adventurers" then sailed into what they called St. George's River (now St. Mary's), where they purchased land, already cleared, from Chief Yacomico with a generous exchange of axes, hoes, and English cloth. Of all the places to settle on the lower Potomac, St. Mary's was the most ideal, located 2 miles up the sheltered St. Mary's River and 4 miles above Point Lookout where the Potomac empties into Chesapeake Bay. St. Mary's would remain the first capital of the new colony for sixty years. When the capital was moved to Annapolis in 1694, the population of St. Mary's City dwindled.

William Claiborne, a Virginia trader, established a small trading colony not far from the mouth of the Patapsco River on Kent Island.

Leonard Calvert, seeking no disagreements with Claiborne, allowed him to stay, but not for long. Claiborne, while on a trip to England, lost his settlement on Kent Island. It was plundered by Leonard Calvert, who then took possession. When Claiborne returned, he promptly saw to it that St. Mary's paid the price.

Claiborne claimed Kent Island as part of Virginia. His small colony on Kent Island was recognized by the Virginia House of Burgesses and was considered one of the first Virginia settlements in the Chesapeake Bay region. King James I and King Charles I had a habit of giving the same lands to different people (originating from faulty maps), causing hostility and occasional bloodshed. Claiborne, with his claim to Kent Island, upheld by the Virginia Council, became the fly in the ointment, by setting the Susquehannocks against the St. Mary's colony. With an accomplice, Richard Ingle, Claiborne pirated Maryland's shipping until forces of Marylanders and Virginians drove him out of the Bay region.

As disputes arose, Maryland was called upon by the Crown to accept changes, few of which favored Maryland. The vast land extending south from Wilmington, Delaware, was given to the Duke of York in 1664 by his brother, King Charles II.

Very few European settlers could be found in western Maryland before 1730. As they moved into western Maryland, a quarrel developed between the Calverts and the Penns over the ownership by Maryland of a 4,000-acre strip of land granted in Lord Baltimore's charter, the boundary line between the two colonies. Between 1732 and 1736, Pennsylvanians and Marylanders conducted retaliatory border raids. Thomas Cresap, then a Maryland guerilla leader, obtained approval through Lord Baltimore's agent and advisor, Daniel Dulany, to conduct several raids. The undeclared war came to an end in 1736 when Cresap was imprisoned by the Pennsylvanians. Later, Dulany secured Cresap's release and they joined together in purchasing huge pieces of land that were resold to settlers. The boundary issue was not settled until 1760. Proprietors of the two colonies contracted with two English surveyors, Charles Mason and Jeremiah Dixon, to fix the boundary. Maryland lost 2.5 million acres of land and major towns like Gettysburg and York. The boundary was finally marked in 1784 by milestones that had Lord Baltimore's coat-of-arms on one side and that of the Penns on the other. It has come to be known as the Mason-Dixon line.

The western and southern boundaries of the Potomac River still remained in dispute. The charter fixed the western boundary of Maryland by first establishing an anchor point described as "the true Meridian of the first Fountain of the River of Pattowmack" (where the river's water first bubbles out of the ground), and from that point, a longitudinal line running northward to its intersection with the 40th degree of latitude. That line, once established, would constitute the western boundary of Maryland. No land description could have been easier to understand. The "first fountain" had to be out there somewhere, and it would have been a simple matter to trace the river to its headspring, its humble beginnings, where the fountain comes out of the ground.

The geography of the Potomac's "first fountain" is of unusual interest. The headspring rises in today's Grant County, West Virginia, then dribbles down a slope, westward. It then makes a three-quarter mile horseshoe turn, flowing east to cross the line of the true meridian, three-quarters of a mile north of the little town of Kempton, Maryland. A stone monument, known as Marker No. 1, now marks the precise point of the southwesternmost corner of Maryland. The Fairfax Stone, near Kempton, Maryland, which marks the point originally chosen as the "first fountain," has great meaning as an historical marker and a reference point in private and public land surveys. Prior to 1910, its location acted as a point to identify the beginning of the 40th degree of north latitude used to establish the southwestern boundary of lands described in Lord Baltimore's Charter of 1632. The location also served as a reference point to identify the western boundary of lands granted to Baron Thomas, Lord Colepeper (Culpeper), from James II in 1688 in connection with the King's granting of the northern neck of Virginia to him. His grant came 56 years after Maryland's charter was granted to Lord Baltimore. Culpeper's western line ran from the headspring of the Potomac south to the "first fountain" of the Rappahannock River.

Lord Culpeper's daughter married into the Fairfax family, and the grant to Lord Culpeper thereafter was simply known as the Fairfax Land Grant. To settle a boundary dispute between the then Lord

Fairfax and the Colony of Virginia, commissioners were appointed, and in September 1736, surveyors proceeded up the Potomac, perpetuating the error of the mislocation of the true headspring of the Potomac by passing by the mouth of the South Branch. The surveying party was appointed by the King of England and was led by Captain Benjamin Winslow and Major William Mayo. After much hardship and near-starvation, the party reached the source of the North Branch. Their job was to determine the northwestern corner of the great Northern Neck Land Tract for Thomas, Virginia's Sixth Lord Fairfax. The party of seventeen surveyors and assistants spent over two months reaching the "first fountain." John Savage was one of the surveyors with the Winslow-Mayo party and received the honor of having the Savage River named after him, becoming the first European to have a geographic feature named after him in Garrett County, Maryland.

Ten years later, on October 22, 1746, Peter Jefferson, father of Thomas Jefferson, and Benjamin Winslow, with a surveyor named Thomas Lewis, arrived at the point where the commissioners, in 1736, had made their marks. In addition to making fresh markings of their own, the party installed the first "Fairfax Stone," shaped like a fist with the initials Fx marked on it. This occurred over 100 years after Lord Baltimore had received his charter. The point marked the boundary of a vast tract of land comprising almost one-fourth of the entire colony of Virginia, which was inherited by Thomas, Sixth Lord Fairfax from his mother, the daughter of Lord Culpeper.

In 1752, at Governor Sharpe's request, Thomas Cresap surveyed both Potomac branches to determine which branch began farther south, the greater distance from the Chesapeake Bay, and therefore, which should be properly identified as the "first fountain of the Potomac." Cresap reported in 1752 that the South Branch was, indeed, the longer of the two branches. If the South Branch claim had been upheld it would have increased the size of Maryland considerably, including today's West Virginia towns of Romney, Moorefield, Petersburg, and Franklin, by placing the source of the South Branch more to the south into today's Commonwealth of Virginia. This would have meant that the revised location of the "first fountain" at the headspring of the South Branch would have been located 133 miles from its confluence with the Potomac, as compared to the 109-mile distance from the most southerly point of the North Branch to the Potomac confluence.

The "first fountain" dispute was finally heard by the Supreme Court in 1910, which refused to correct the error. The Supreme Court invoked the common-law doctrine of prescription and adverse possession to settle the issue. Henceforth, the Fairfax Stone site on the North Branch would remain the "first fountain" of the Potomac, even though its location differed from the intended charter description. So, the Fairfax Stone would continue to mark the place where the courts, the states, and the public would finally accept the stone as the historic point where the Potomac has its beginnings.

In all, five stones have been installed at the Fairfax Spring to mark the location of the famous landmark that later became known as the Fairfax Stone. Stones number four and five still stand today. The fourth is an obelisk cast in concrete with 1910 incised on the north side and Fx and 1746 on the south side. The fifth stone is the 6-ton boulder brought to the site from the mountains near Davis, West Virginia, and placed directly over the Fairfax Spring. A bronze plaque is embedded into the top of the boulder and reads:

This monument, at the headspring of the Potomac River, marks one of the historic spots in America. Its name is derived from Thomas Lord Fairfax who owned all the land lying between the Potomac and Rappahannock rivers. The first Fairfax Stone marked "FX" was set in 1746 by Thomas Lewis, a surveyor employed by Lord Fairfax. This is the base point for the western dividing line between Maryland and West Virginia.

THE PUSH WEST

As European settlers moved westward, they became aware that virtually the entire eastern part of the country was criss-crossed with Indian trails, usually unmarked, following mountain ridges, valleys, and streams. Most were narrow pathways, except for the ancient buffalo traces that were thought by many to be highly functional, almost engineered. Many of these paths joined others, stretching routes for hundreds of miles. Wagon roads were built over existing paths to accommodate freight, passengers, and military wagons. Broad-wheeled,

The fourth Fairfax Stone, cast in concrete, was installed in 1910 at the Fairfax spring and still stands today. (Photo by Richard Stanton)

covered Conestoga wagons, manufactured in Lancaster County, Pennsylvania, were common sights along the freight trails.

Packhorse Ford was one of the most important Potomac River crossings, located about 1.5 miles below the present-day Rumsey Bridge at Shepherdstown, West Virginia. Prior to the appearance of Europeans in the region, the ford was part of the famous "Warrior Path," running northeast-southwest, and for many years, was the main route between the Iroquois and the Cherokees. It is believed that Louis Michel, a Swiss traveler who visited and mapped the Potomac Valley in 1707, crossed Packhorse Ford. Five years later, the

This 6-ton boulder was brought to the site from the mountains near Davis, West Virginia, and was placed directly over the spring. It is the fifth Fairfax Stone. Dedicated on October 5, 1957. (Photo by Richard Stanton)

Swiss baron, Christoph de Graffenried, is thought to have crossed here on his way to the northern portion of the Shenandoah Valley seeking settlement sites for Swiss Moravians.

As early as 1726, Germans from Pennsylvania began to cross the Potomac at Packhorse Ford in significant numbers. Many settled between the ford and "Apple Pie Ridge," several miles northwest of the ford, near the Opequon River. By 1730 a settlement grew near the ford called Mecklinburg (Shepherdstown). Chartered in 1767, it became the oldest town within the present limits of West Virginia. In 1796, the name was changed to Shepherd's Town in honor of its patron, Thomas Shepherd. During the 1730s and until shortly after 1800, the Potomac River crossings at Harpers Ferry and Mecklinburg were the most important along the upper Potomac River, bringing German, Swiss, Irish, Welsh, and Scots-Irish to settle.

For a number of years, a lucrative fur trade flourished between the French and the Indians in the Ohio Valley. By 1749, a group of

Maryland and Virginia citizens began sharing in this trade, causing tensions with its boasts that the Ohio Company would become the "vanguard of the British advance into the Ohio Country." The Ohio Company's charter included 200,000 acres of land, with a promise of 300,000 more acres if a fort was built in the Ohio country and 200 families would move in. The Ohio Company decided to build its fort at the "forks of the Ohio," where the Monongahela and Allegheny rivers meet. Work on the fort was postponed and, instead, the company built a "trading warehouse" on the Potomac at Wills Creek.

In the meantime, the Ohio Company hired Thomas Cresap and the famous Delaware Indian explorer Nemacolin in 1751 to survey a road between Wills Creek and the "forks of the Ohio." A 65-mile portage was marked that provided a link between the Ohio and Potomac rivers.

Major General Edward Braddock arrived at Wills Creek on May 10, 1755, and promptly renamed the new fort Fort Cumberland, in honor of the Duke of Cumberland, son of George II and the Captain General of the British army. General Braddock had been sent from England to command the British forces in America. His ill-trained and poorly supplied army would soon be called upon to march to Fort Duquesne on the Ohio and attempt to force most of the French troops back to Canada to prepare the way for English settlement of the Ohio. The French and Indian War ended in 1763, but the events surrounding Braddock's death and the reality of Indian raiding parties had a depressing effect on all western settlement. Settlers in the Wills Creek/Fort Cumberland areas fled east to escape the threat of Indian attacks. Not only did settlers flee from Wills Creek, but from most of the Potomac Valley, from South Mountain westward. For several years settlers stayed away to return only when unrest subsided and lands could be protected by the militia.

One more attempt to push west came with the authorization of the federally funded National Road, which resulted from the admission of Ohio as a state in 1802. The enabling legislation signed by Thomas Jefferson in 1808 provided for 2 percent of the sale of public lands in Ohio to go for a road to tie that state with other states in the Union.

With the advance of the settlers and the need to open roads for the movement of manufactured goods to be traded for farm products, several major wagon roads were constructed to the Ohio and beyond. The old Braddock Road from Cumberland to the Monongahela River, built by General Edward Braddock in 1755, was widened and pressed into service. In 1797, the Baltimore National Pike was opened, running from Baltimore to Cumberland, the easternmost section of the National Road. The Great Philadelphia Wagon Road accommodated wagons to and from Philadelphia, through York, Pennsylvania, along the present Route 30 to the present Route 11, then through the Shenandoah Valley. Daniel Boone's Wilderness Road branched off from the Philadelphia Road half way through Virginia and proceeded west to Cumberland Gap.

The National Road was completed to Wheeling in 1818, built by the United States government, following the same trail used earlier by Cresap, Nemacolin, frontiersman and military scout Christopher Gist, and General Braddock. It has been estimated that nearly a thousand freight wagons crossed the road between Cumberland and Wheeling the first year of its operation. Routes of communication were opened beyond the Ohio and commerce was now assured.

Chapter 4.

WASHINGTON'S
PATOWMACK COMPANY

The origins of the Potomac Company, George Washington's pet project, a chartered interstate organization to develop navigation on the Potomac, date to the mid-eighteenth century, when traders loaded their boats with goods and journeyed down the Potomac River to reach eager markets in Georgetown and beyond. Their voyage covered vast distances by pole and oar. At nightfall, cargo was hidden, out of sight of raiders who would not have hesitated to attack the traders and steal their cargoes.

Trading brought enormous profits, but not without risk. The dangers of river travel on the Potomac were well known. Despite these difficulties, a brisk and lucrative trade was developed along the Potomac. Boat loads of trade goods from as far upriver as Westernport, Maryland, 226 river-miles above tidewater, were floated downstream for sale or trade. Furs were much in demand and were brought down from as far west as the Ohio frontier, then trans-shipped to European ports. To reach tidewater where the markets were, goods had to be laboriously unloaded and carried around the most dangerous barriers, causing great time loss and hazards to the cargoes.

Shorter freight hauls were also made, especially after coal was first discovered just west of Cumberland at Barrelville. Most coal loads were sold out by the time the boats reached the falls above Harpers Ferry so great was the demand. All this was happening long before the Potomac Company received its charter in 1784.

Enterprising individuals were engaged in an expanding fur trade along the rivers. Beaver and other fine pelts were collected at "factorages," or posts, where the government would exchange goods with Indians for furs, such as Fort Osage on the Missouri River, and Fort Madison on the upper Mississippi River. Furs were brought down these two rivers to St. Louis, then down the Mississippi and up the Ohio River to Wheeling in all manner of freight boats. From Wheeling it was an arduous 120-mile overland haul to Fort Cumberland; the furs were again loaded onto boats and taken down the Potomac to the wharves at Georgetown where they were received by the Superintendent of Indian Trade. In all, it was a difficult 2,000-mile journey. One cannot imagine the great hardships, intense labor, and dangers of a trip of this length; yet trade was increasing and the more complex and difficult the haul, the higher the prices. Impassable falls, rocks, and dangerous rapids impeded freight handling on all rivers. Improvements along the water routes did not seem feasible, nor were they expected.

The Potomac, as a river of commerce, beckoned many daring adventurers. Attempts to subdue the wild Potomac were vigorously promoted. Schemes were advanced to transform the rocky and turbulent river into an access route to and from the West. Adventurous exploits to exchange trade goods from eastern settlements for return goods from the Ohio settlements and beyond were undertaken by entrepreneurial boat owners.

The Potomac River, for all its potential, seemingly remained elusive to such exploitive schemes. There wasn't enough money anywhere, public or private, to engage in precipitous adventures that knew no precedent. Few in this country had ever seen a canal or a lock, yet, in the typical and flamboyant manner of the day, there were those who were willing to experiment, learning hard lessons along the way. Each successive attempt to subdue the great barriers on the Potomac would add knowledge and experience to be passed on to those ambitious and brave enough to follow. Simply navigating the Potomac and Shenandoah river routes without losing cargo and crew was challenge enough, but to attempt to tame these wild waters from beginning to end was an enigma seemingly beyond reach in the mid-eighteenth century.

From Westernport, there were three major impediments to river travel in high water: Shenandoah Falls in the Potomac at Harpers Ferry, Great Falls, and Little Falls. George Washington, in a letter to Thomas Lee, dated August 1754, gave an account of a canoe trip he took down the Potomac to investigate the potential for navigating the river. Washington was 22-years-old at the time. The letter read:

Sir:

Your desire, added to my own curiosity engaged me the last time I was in Frederick to return down by water to discover the navigation of the Potowmack; following are the observations I made thereupon in that trip. From the mouth of Patersons Creek [13 miles below Cumberland] to the begg. of Shenandoah Falls [in the Potomac at Harpers Ferry, a distance of 122 river-miles] there is no other obstacle than the shallowness of the water to prevent Craft from passing . . .

In January 1755, during the French and Indian War, Governor Horatio Sharpe of Maryland, and Sir John St. Clair, Major General Edward Braddock's commissary general, left Fort Cumberland on a 183-mile exploratory mission down the Potomac River to Great Falls to determine whether military supplies could be better carried upriver in boats than by wagon trains. After examining the 77-foot drop at Great Falls, St. Clair thought the idea would be feasible only if the rocks under the falls could be blasted away to allow British ships to load at the base of the falls. The idea of transporting military supplies upriver by boat was subsequently abandoned.

St. Clair proceeded to Alexandria where he joined General Braddock, who had just arrived with 2,000 British troops, eager to move upriver to trounce the French in western Pennsylvania at Fort Duquesne. Braddock viewed, with contempt, the addition of the untrained colonial militia to his charge, which included the ubiquitous Colonel George Washington of Virginia. Braddock's arrogance and ineptitude may have contributed to the defeat of the British by the French in a fierce battle fought on July 9, 1755, less than 10 miles from Fort Duquesne. Washington survived the battle, while Sir John

St. Clair was seriously wounded. General Braddock was killed and buried in an anonymous grave under the very road that had been built under his orders and had carried his troops and wagons to his ill-fated fight with the French. Had the French followed up their victory they might have taken all of Maryland. But the northern colonies began to attack the French, who were eventually compelled to withdraw most of their troops back to Canada. These events might have greatly changed the course of American history, sounding the death-knell for any American plans to use the Potomac River as a link to the Ohio and Mississippi river valleys.

In December 1769, George Washington, then a member of the Virginia House of Burgesses, presented a bill to the assembly for clearing rocks from the Potomac River from upriver to tidewater, to make the Potomac navigable. Richard Henry Lee co-sponsored the bill. Concurrently, Thomas Johnson, a member of the Maryland legislature, made an attempt to convince the Maryland Assembly to pass a similar act, but Baltimore merchants who would not benefit economically saw to it that the act went nowhere.

Meanwhile, independent attempts to tame the river were making some progress. An ingenious method of moving boats up or down the Potomac River was devised by John Ballendine in about 1770. Ballendine, intending to operate a sawmill at the foot of Seneca Falls, 6 miles above the Great Falls cataract, actually built two dams across the natural channels between Watkins Island and the Virginia shoreline with 4-foot gates at the base of each pool. A third pool with a third gate would have had a lift sufficient to raise the river level above the Seneca Falls. This latter scheme had the potential for accommodating boats from above Great Falls upriver to Paynes Falls, located 5 miles above the town of Berlin (now Brunswick). Had there been a sufficient number of boats available to make it worthwhile, commercial navigation from above Great Falls might have been pursued.

In 1777, Ballendine advanced a plan, which had wide public support, to make the Potomac navigable from tidewater to above Fort Cumberland. Convinced that his ideas were sound, he traveled to Europe where he examined inland systems of navigation in England and France. While in London he requested permission to solicit stock subscriptions for a major project that would enable him to begin work at Shenandoah Falls in the Potomac River, above Harpers Ferry, and continue work already started on the Potomac's "lower falls" (Little Falls). Ballendine returned from Europe with skilled craftsmen who were engaged to begin work on the Potomac River. Subscribers for the project were successfully recruited. One of the subscribers was George Washington, who understood and supported Ballendine's proposal. Ballendine's minimum depth would be at least 4 feet. Part of his plan was to build a lock stairway through the "gut" (center) of the Great Falls with no less than eight locks to overcome the 77-foot fall. Freight boats would be designed to carry an astonishing 150 to 200 tons of cargo. His plan was short-lived, however. The Revolutionary War eclipsed his ambitious agenda and his plan was never revived.

Although General Charles Cornwallis surrendered his army to General George Washington at Yorktown in 1781, ending the Revolutionary War, two years elapsed before peace was realized. On November 25, 1783, Washington's army drove the last of the British out of New York amidst the sounds of booming cannons and great cheering. After an emotional farewell to his officers at Fraunces Tavern on December 23, Washington proceeded to Annapolis where the Congress was then seated. Before a multitude of spectators, and after a brief but eloquent address, he resigned his commission as Commander-in-Chief of the American forces into the hands of the then president of the Congress and became a private citizen. When the ceremony concluded, he rode south at a hard gallop with three of his aides, reaching Mount Vernon in time for dinner on Christmas Eve 1783.

After the ordeal of the Revolutionary War, Washington's fervent desire was to spend the remainder of his days "cultivating the affections of good men and in the practice of domestic virtues." Although he was 52, there was still ample time to get his life in order, experiment with his crops, and most of all, resume his role as the master of Mount Vernon. His days were full and there was always unfinished business to be taken care of.

It was inevitable that his thoughts would eventually return to his western landholdings and the ridges of the Alleghenies with which he was so familiar. In September 1784, Washington set off on a journey to inspect his lands in the Ohio Valley and to examine the river systems flowing east and west. He also wanted to examine the pace and extent of interior trade. Washington was warned not to proceed on his journey, but he departed nevertheless. Washington's nephew, Bushrod, his personal physician Dr. James Craik and his son, James Jr., and three attendants accompanied him on the journey. It proved exhausting and involved great hardship. During the war, many migrant families had settled beyond the ridges into the Ohio territories. To conform with the Articles of Confederation, both Maryland and Virginia ceded lands to the United States. Although the Confederation was now sovereign, it lacked the power to govern, causing many problems. Indians and settlers in the Ohio territories were fighting each other.

Washington visited with inventor James Rumsey as he passed through Bath (Berkeley Springs), having heard of Rumsey's ingenious experiments, "working boats against the stream by mechanical levers, principally." Washington considered James Rumsey's experiments of vast importance. They might well play a role in Potomac navigation, and prove to be the means of reaching "The Grand Emporium," as Washington called the lands to the west. From Bath, Washington passed through Fort Cumberland on his way to the highest ridges of the Allegheny summit, at the headwaters of the Potomac and Ohio rivers. With characteristic wisdom, he foresaw the rapid settlement of the Ohio Valley and the upper Mississippi River Valley. The mouth of the Mississippi was then in the hands of the Spanish, and there was the likelihood that Spain would capture the western trade. There was also a probability that vast populations would be separated if nothing was done to assure commercial navigation of the western rivers. What was more, western North Carolina (now Tennessee) had no water outlet to the sea except by way of the Mississippi. North Carolina was in a mood to open negotiations with Spain to form an alliance that could doom any eastern linkage with these two potentially great commercial connections.

Washington was convinced that access to the Ohio River was practical by proceeding to the highest navigable point on the Potomac, then crossing Backbone Mountain by road and descending to the headwaters of the Cheat River. From there, boats could proceed down the Monongahela and Ohio rivers and travel as far north as the Great Lakes. Washington's detailed knowledge of the watershed lands of the Ohio and Potomac river valleys, and their accompanying river systems, served his country well. Even as a young surveyor in the employ of Colonel George William Fairfax he had roamed these high ridge lands with his father's surveying chain and compass. As a colonel in the Virginia Militia, he had accompanied Braddock in the disastrous campaign against the French. It was through these experiences that Washington gained his understanding of the region's potential.

On his 1784 journey, Washington saw clearly that the time was right to take action on his Potomac navigation idea. It was the first in a series of vast internal improvements that would bind the young nation together, establish communication between communities, and expand and enlarge commerce. Washington's probe into the Potomac and Ohio headwaters lasted almost five weeks and covered some 700 miles in the saddle at his usual gait of 5 miles per hour. Washington returned home by way of Staunton, Virginia, to investigate the upper Shenandoah River system. He believed that navigation could be extended from Port Republic, Virginia, by the middle fork of the mouth of Lewis Creek, 20 river-miles distant and only 6 miles by land from Staunton. With this accomplishment, the Shenandoah River could be made navigable for 220 miles to Harpers Ferry. Had it been fully realized, it would have been the second longest water route in the Potomac River system.

It has been asserted that Washington's principal reason for opening trade to the West by way of the Potomac River was to seek a good route to his personal western landholdings. If this had been so he would most likely have decided on the James-Kanawha river routes, as his lands, for the most part, were in that direction.

I wish that every individual who may hear that it was a favorite plan of mine, may know also that I had no other motive for promoting it than the advantage of which I conceived it would be productive to the Union at large and to this state in particular, by cementing the eastern and western territory together. At the same time it will give vigor and increase to our commerce and be a convenience to our citizens. (George Washington)

Upon his return to Mount Vernon, Washington devised a bold plan. Writing to Governor Harrison of Virginia, he summed up his plan:

. . . extend the inland navigation of the eastern waters, communicate them as near as possible by excellent roads with those which run to the westward. Open these to the Ohio and such others as extend from the Ohio toward Lake Erie; and we shall not only draw the produce of the western settlers but the fur and peltry trade of the Lakes also to our ports.

Both Virginia and Maryland claimed portions of the Potomac River to be within their boundary jurisdictions. Washington appeared before the Virginia legislature in 1784, presenting his navigation plan and requesting a charter for the Potomac Company. At the same time, James Madison presented Washington's plan to the Maryland Assembly. Committees were formed and each state showed support by subscribing 10 percent of the stock. With such beloved and revered luminaries as Washington and James Madison behind the formation of the Potomac Company, matters finally moved quickly.

In March 1785, appointed commissioners met at Mount Vernon. Virginia and Maryland recommended that the states adopt systems of duties, regulations, and rules regarding currency. An agreement was made, known as the Compact of 1785, or the Mount Vernon Compact. Among other articles, the Potomac River was to be a common highway. Citizens owning property in both states would be at liberty to transport their produce duty-free. Riparian rights and fishing rights were to be common to citizens on both sides of the river. Hence, the compact violated the Articles of Confederation, which prohibited states from entering into any foreign treaties, alliances, or confederations. There was the delicate subject of interstate trade to consider if Potomac navigation was to become a reality. Trade goods from Ohio had to pass through Pennsylvania, down a Maryland river, then be delivered to ports in Virginia and Maryland. Further, the Articles of Confederation provided that existing states would operate independently, with their own powers to tax and with their own currencies. Subsequently, the Potomac Company was boldly chartered by both Maryland and Virginia in 1784–1785. A constitutional convention would have to be assembled to deal with the infringements to the Articles of Confederation presented by the formation of the Potomac Company, but in the meantime there was much work to be done.

The first meeting of the Potomac Company was held in the city of Alexandria on May 17, 1785. George Washington was elected president. John Fitzgerald and George Gilpin, prominent Alexandria businessmen, and the Honorable Thomas Sim Lee and Thomas Johnson, esquires, both former Maryland governors, were made directors of the company. Books for the subscription of stock were opened with shares totaling 403, having a capital value £40,300 sterling. Discussions ensued on the best way to divide up the work at hand on the river, how to obtain the services of skillful workers, and compensation to be disbursed by the treasurer, William Hartshorne, and the clerk of the company, John Pitt, Jr.

A constitutional convention was finally assembled in 1787, in Philadelphia, to resolve the critical problems of interstate commerce presented by the formation of the Potomac Company. It called for a new form of government, rallying to Alexander Hamilton's call "to devise such further provisions as should appear to them necessary to render the constitution of the federal government adequate to the exigencies of the Union." The Constitution was adopted and thus, citizens of the United States would now be able to engage in interstate commerce without taxes or duties being imposed on goods transported from one state to, or through, another state. Washington's hopes and aspirations were, at last, being realized. The Potomac River would be the first of many common highways that would bind the nation. The Congress seemed ready to administer national affairs independently from the states.

According to the terms of its charter, from 1785 to 1828, the purpose of the Potomac Company was to open the Potomac River to the highest point of permanent navigation and included clearing the river of rocks, building bypass locks and canals, building and maintaining sluiceways and wing walls to guide the water into channels, and constructing other navigational works. All works were to be built so that boats would have a minimum clearance of 1 foot of water. Inventor

James Rumsey was appointed superintendent of the Potomac Company. He was considered the most promising candidate on a slate of several. River navigation with its sluiceways and locks was a new and untried technology in this emerging nation, and it is doubtful that anyone more suited to the task could have been found on this side of the Atlantic. Rumsey was an exceptional mechanic and boat builder. Washington had a favorable opinion of Rumsey and lobbied for him, taking the lead in seeing to it that Rumsey would be considered for the position. He was selected with a starting salary of £200 a year. Richardson Stewart was selected as Rumsey's assistant manager at £120. Rumsey knew the river well and took the lead in introducing the directors and stockholders to the most strategic points where works might be installed. "Guts" (narrow passages) and "swashes" (bodies of swift dashing water) were examined in detail for their navigational potential. Major falls like the "Spout" (White Horse Rapid), below Harpers Ferry along the Maryland shore, were studied.

The Potomac Company was required to provide for navigation of waters 1-foot deep or more, throughout the year. This threshold requirement was expected to be met under its charter and was to have been the key to the river's low-water navigability. All works were designed and constructed to meet the minimum 1-foot depth. This design requirement for a river full of rocks and ledges is perplexing. Obviously, the design of the Potomac Company's river works were greatly influenced by French and English waterway designs with their virtually quiet, rock-free waters. British canals were chiefly lined with clay or marl (mixtures), covered with gravel and rocks that shifted with every movement of the bed course. English and French works were also subject to flooding, bank breaks, and damage from freshets. For the boatmen, strong and reliable freshets provided the safest, fastest, and most satisfactory means of making successful near-flood trips downriver in only three or four days of river travel with assurance that at the end of the voyage, good progress could be made by hauling the boat, return cargo and crew, back to its point of origin in seven to eight days. Thus, for purposes of upriver travel, the desirable characteristic of a freshet was its sudden drop in water level. To have run down the river in high and continuous flood would have meant that crews would have been required to spend nonpro-

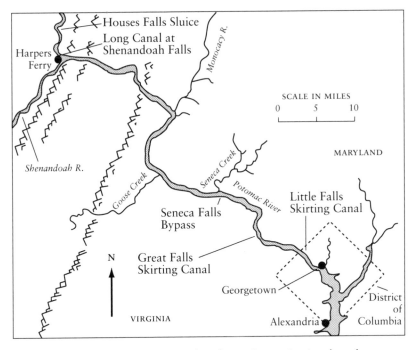

Route of the Potomac Company and its five major navigational works.

ductive days at the tidewater end of the run, impatiently awaiting an abatement in the water level. Hauling a light and profitable return load avoided idleness at any point along the journey, resulting in larger returns on the boat owner's investment and fewer days to feed hungry mouths. Tolls were high, and margins of profit always speculative. The boat owners and their handlers took no unnecessary chances. Boats were as much as 75 feet in length and 8 feet wide, and full of surprises.

Understandably, the story of the Potomac Company's primitive works on both sides of the Potomac River and the later works of the Chesapeake and Ohio Canal Company along the Maryland shore, cause confusion in the minds of some who may not have sorted out the differences in these two great projects, which seem to be similar in many respects.

To understand the Potomac Company project (1785 to 1828), we

High water and hazards. (Photo by Richard Stanton)

On Saturday, October 9, 1976, I became a reincarnated eighteenth-century river boatman. It started innocently enough. My three companions and I were poised to take a fall colors trip down the Potomac from Oldtown to Hancock, Maryland. The following story comes straight from my canoe journals, a harrowing tale of fear and near-drowning.

The night before, we had set up a cozy camp on Pumper Island, just below the Oldtown low-water bridge. The Potomac River was overflowing from continuing rains, and more was expected. We had hoped the river would crest that night, but instead it rained harder with no let-up. During the night, I nervously shined my flashlight at the shoreline at intervals to keep track of the rising water levels.

At daybreak, I discovered to my horror that the river was only 6 feet from my tent. I sounded the alarm. It was rising fast. As it turned out, the river covered the island less than 30 minutes later. One of my companions was determined to make coffee but the flood waters began swirling around our small stove, eventually extinguishing the flame. We quickly broke camp and gathered our scattered gear, then jumped into the canoes. Without warning, the rising waters threatened to lift our canoes and gear off the island within minutes. We were swiftly drawn into the center of the swollen river, slowly spinning inside trash piles, floating alongside logs, flotsam, foam cups, bleach bottles, and steel drums. Three days of rain in the upper valley had set the stage for a good old-fashioned Patowmack Company freshet, giving us a chance to test a few theories we had about river speeds and the dangers of high-high freshet water levels.

My canoe moved quickly, nested in that raft of circling trash. A 100-gallon drum was my traveling companion for several miles. I felt like a discarded cereal box as we made a fast approach to Town Creek. The water was a muddy brown, water from which there would be no return in an upset. My maps were marked in miles. Checking our speed, we were pressing forward at a rate of 9 miles an hour. For the uninitiated, 9 miles an hour on the river is an awesome speed in an open canoe with no place to land safely. The conditions we were experiencing were identical to those of the early boatmen. This freshet was at medium-flood stage. Almost anything could have happened. Once in the center of a river's powerful flow, release is unlikely. Submerged trees preclude any chance of pulling to shore successfully without great risk to boat and paddler. Flailing through "keeper" trees seemingly guarantees a rollover or a broadsiding into any immovable obstruction. It's "lights out" if control of the canoe is lost! A steady, gripping, unwavering course down the center of the river with the other cereal boxes is safest, but recurring immovable railroad piers beckoned around every turn. The canoes were strung out for a couple of miles. Many times we were out of sight of one another. Our grand plan was to have the lead canoe land and wait, but we couldn't tell if anyone was in front or in back of our boats. We continued at 9 miles an hour. Aqueducts built to carry canal water across the mouths of rivers were covered, and it was difficult to determine where we were at any given time, so inundated were our usual familiar landmarks.

As I sped under the Paw Paw Bridge, I couldn't believe what I saw out of the corner of my eye: my friend of many years, John Seabury Thomson, and several companions getting ready to put their boats into the turbulent waters. In addition to my companions, I now had John and his crew to worry about. John wrote of his adventure in the club newsletter, *The Canoe Cruiser,* soon after. He described the river as moving at "express-train speed." I learned that he had thinned out the number of canoes in his group, winding up with seven experienced stalwarts. His two-day outing took only three hours on the water.

After two hours and almost 20 miles, I spied two of my companions ahead scrambling up a bank to higher ground, dragging their loaded boats behind them. All was not well. Our fourth canoe was missing. I finally spied the lost canoeist racing downriver in the center of a 40-foot trash raft. We both managed to land, pulling our canoes to the top of a high hill where the whole party regrouped. We had good food and sufficient comforts for two nights, so all was well.

In a freshet it's each person for himself. The Potomac boatmen of the past would not have propelled their boats beyond the speed of the river for fear of losing control and broadsiding into submerged trees at turns in the river. At the rate we had been going, we could have reached Harpers Ferry by nightfall, and Great Falls, 15 miles from the Georgetown wharves, by noon the following day.

Two days later, on October 11, we beat a hasty retreat, speeding down the river to Hancock, 30 miles in less than four hours. On the next day, the water was dropping at the rate of 5 to 7 feet a day and was soon back within its banks. For those who may be interested, on the day before the freshet trip, the Hancock gauge was at 5.5 feet. On the day of the freshet run, October 10, the gauge had risen to 26.3 feet. On Sunday, October 11, the gauge was down 4 feet to 22.3 feet—a classic freshet any boatman would have given his weekly whiskey ration for.

At the conclusion of the four-day run, one of my companions said, "I wouldn't have missed this great experience for 85 cents!" We had truly been riders of the freshet, but, mercifully, we didn't have to pole our way back to Cumberland to pick up another 15 tons of big-vein coal for Admiral Dewey's navy.

---

must contemplate the intended functions of its primitive works, both in the river and along the banks of the river. Freight was loaded into shallow draft longboats owned by enterprising boat captains and floated and poled downriver to unloading points. The longboats were literally hauled back to the point of origin by the crew, which pulled, pushed, and poled the boats upriver. Depending on the resistance of the downriver water, the return to Cumberland could take as long as ten days, or more. The work was dangerous and the river could only be used on an average of some six weeks a year, during periods of high water freshets. Sometimes cargoes overturned and lives were lost, but it was still a way to make a good living during that period in the nation's history.

The Potomac Company built five major works: (1) the 2.17-mile Little Falls Skirting Canal on the Maryland side of the river, with four locks, dropping the river a distance of 37.2 feet; (2) the Great Falls Skirting Canal on the Virginia side of the river, with five locks, and a fall of 76.9 feet; (3) Seneca Falls Bypass toward the right center of the river, a drop of 7 feet in .75 mile; (4) the Long Canal at Shenandoah Falls alongside the Potomac on the Maryland bank, located a mile above Harpers Ferry Gap (the Long Canal was a 1-mile-long skirting canal, running from the top of what is now known as C & O Canal's Dam No. 3 to its outlet, at the Potomac and Shenandoah confluence, having a total drop of 15 feet); and (5) the Houses Falls sluice, located 5 miles upriver from Harpers Ferry, at a length of 50 yards with a drop of 3 feet. In their time, these larger works and the many miscellaneous river improvements were considered major engineering feats, making the Potomac Company story a fascinating and important engineering accomplishment beyond compare, not only for its stockholders, but for a young and developing nation eager to move forward and experiment with untested transportation possibilities.

Potomac Company President John Mason, in his report to Secretary of the Treasury, Albert Gallatin, in 1808, discussed the errors made in constructing the Potomac Company works, admitting the lack of practical knowledge in the early stages of the project. For example, improper wood was used in three of the Little Falls locks, and all four locks were oversized, causing a loss of time and work in filling them. These and other defects were eventually remedied, but not without a loss of revenue and time. In reading through the report, it becomes evident that Mason was overwhelmed with the scope and daring of the project, calling it ". . . this great work."

THIS GREAT WORK:
THE POTOMAC COMPANY RIVER WORKS

Houses Falls Sluice

Moving down the Potomac River, the first major Potomac Company work was located at Houses Falls, 5 miles above Harpers Ferry on the former Virginia side of the river. It can still be seen from the C & O Canal towpath on the Maryland side of the river near Milepost 66. Ahead, below a bend in the river, is an island crossing diagonally toward the former Virginia side of the river. Here lies Houses Falls, known today as Fishpot Falls, or sometimes River Bend Falls.

In Washington's time the Houses Falls area was called Caton's Gut. Here is one of the finest examples of sluice navigation on any river. Sluice navigation is the technique of introducing a boat straight into a level, artificial channel of uniform depth, eliminating obstructions, contrary to a fall (waterfall), which allows for an unrestricted drop of river water of varying heights and depths with no confinement or blocking. The sluice was cut through limestone along the Virginia bank where there now exists the quiet little community of River Bend. The sluice has a 3-foot drop and is only 50 yards long. It is 10-feet deep and fed by water running along a diagonal rock formation moving across the upper edge of the island, sending half the river's rushing water into the upriver end of the sluice, providing good boat passage at any time of year. The sluice was cut along the margin of the river in the fall of 1769, six years before the Potomac Company received its charter. It was cut when John Semple owned the Keep Tryst iron furnace located 5 miles downstream at Harpers Ferry. Semple transported his pig-iron (crude iron as it comes out of the furnace), upriver through the sluice, then continued upriver to Two Wives Island (now known as Knotts Island), across the river from the mouth of Antietam Creek. Semple would deposit the ore on the island and the workers at the Antietam Iron Works would then haul it across the river as they needed it. It was known as Cow Ring Sluice and became an important adjunct to Semple's iron furnace operation. His ore was of the finest quality and in much demand.

In high water, the force of the current rushing down Cow Ring Sluice required the assistance of a capstan (winch) placed on shore at

Houses Falls sluice. (Photo by Richard Stanton)

the top of the sluice to assist in drawing boats upstream. The use of capstans was quite common along the river to assist descending and ascending boats. For some reason, folks at River Bend do not identify this location as Houses Falls. Its pedigree as a sluice used by Potomac Company longboats is generally unknown. The reason seems obvious. Cow Ring Sluice was cut by John Semple, not the Potomac Company, to enable his boats to bypass Houses Falls on the way to and from the mouth of Antietam Creek. It was roughly cut through limestone and has been virtually maintenance-free all these years.

John House owned "Two Wives" (Knotts Island), which was purchased by John Semple from House's heir. The name "Houses Falls" is not found on historic or recent maps. I was introduced to Houses Falls during a solo canoe trip from Cumberland to Washington in 1984. When my map showed the through voyage to be exactly 5 miles above Harper Ferry, there it all was before me. I could see the water running fast toward the top of the sluice along the river bank and it appeared to be deep enough for a passage. Knotts Quarry was just to the west behind the stone wall that protected the sluice on what was then the Virginia side of the river. The top of the sluice is capped with thick limestone blocks. This was Houses Falls to be sure.

While being loaded, stone barges were secured to a thick, heavy limestone platform on which the stone was dumped awaiting loading. The rope or chain rings are still there. The loading platform stones are in excellent condition, but a careful examination of the stone platform above the sluice reveals that it did not exist when the Potomac Company operated through the sluiceway. Longboats would not have loaded or unloaded at this precarious place. Later, this is where Knotts' workers loaded their stone, traveled downriver to the C & O Canal's Dam No. 3, then continued through a guard lock and further transport up or down the C & O Canal to the intended destination.

The Potomac Company must have enlarged Houses Falls sluice to accommodate its wider boats when the company began operations in 1775. Although the cut had already been made, the rights granted under the Potomac Company's charter certainly must have placed the river sluice under the Potomac Company's jurisdiction. A thorough examination of the sluiceway reveals it to be wide enough to accommodate the widest of the Potomac Company's keelboats. The outer edge of the sluice is uniform. The bed of the sluice is level, as evidenced by the full, but tight, wave action at its surface. Few people in those days, including John Semple, would have taken the time to over-build a primitive work of this kind, so its seems reasonable to assume that the Potomac Company improved its function. The width and depth of the sluice would have been the minimum required to accommodate Semple's ore boats. The evidence of the later improvement of this sluice by the Potomac Company may well lie in its excellent craftsmanship.

In addition to building numerous sluiceways, the company built walls in the river to better collect water and confine boats. Low dams would be built across the river from shore to shore, made of river-worn cobbles of a size that laborers could conveniently handle. Walls were 10 to 20 feet in width and were 18 to 24 inches in height. They were built along the shoreline or in suitable locations in the river where the flow could be well contained. A passage, or gap, in the transverse dam at the top of the walling area was provided for boat entry. The gaps forced the current of the river to deepen the channel between the walls.

The technique of walling should not be confused with sluice navigation, which was more permanent and could be used to overcome short lengths of river. Most sluiceways were self-scouring and required little maintenance. The river-miles below the mouth of the Savage River reveal the remnants of walls that were more prevalent at this upper elevation because of the overall shallowness of the river. "Walling" did not work well and the scheme was of little practical consequence. The walls in the river were too fragile and would not remain tight. In fact, the greater number of the longboat wrecks occurred in walled areas, according to information gathered years ago along the river. Dashing the sides of the boats against sluice walls, or bilging, often occurred, as boats were guided along with other boats in rushing waters, and the steersmen would loose control in the walled areas. They were simply built too long.

At the time John Semple cut Cow Ring Sluice for his Keep Tryst iron ore deliveries to Antietam furnace, he probably knew more about river navigation from Shepherdstown to Great Falls than anyone alive. He and John Ballendine were Washington's trusted confidants on Potomac River matters. It was not unusual for Semple, or Ballendine, to visit Washington at Mount Vernon to discuss Potomac River commerce and other ideas. It seems certain that either Semple or Ballendine did the channel cutting at the top of Shenandoah Falls (now top of Dam No. 3) before 1785; most likely it was Ballendine as Semple did not usually engage in speculative endeavors. Much correspondence passed between Washington, Semple, and Ballendine about the river. Semple's ideas were always practical, based on a thorough knowledge of the river's flow and its vagaries. Washington paid attention to Semple, while he found Ballendine's ideas more theoretical and grandiose.

The use of Cow Ring Sluice by the Potomac Company must have been taken for granted by all parties, as the record is silent on whether or not compensation for the work done on the sluice was ever paid to John Semple.

The area from Harpers Ferry Gap to Shepherdstown during colonial days was considered to have prime industrial potential. This was already an enclave of factories with a government armory below a natural dam at the top of Shenandoah Falls, the vast iron ore banks on both sides of the river above Harpers Ferry, the iron works at Antietam, and the Reynolds' flour mill, later converted to Boteler's hydraulic lime cement mill, serving the C & O Canal so well in later years. In addition, there were numerous smaller cement and lime kilns in the vicinity.

In the busy days of the old C & O, a fully loaded stone barge operated by canal barge operator John Houser left the loading dock at Cow Ring Sluice and slowly sank as it attempted to reach the opposite shore in the vicinity of Canal Milepost 63, above Dam No. 3. In low water, the inquisitive can see the outlines of the barge under water. The limestone was left where it sank, perhaps as many as 90 years ago. Cow Ring Sluice is still run today by canoeists and even by motorized pontoon float boats that can navigate up or down the 14-foot-wide sluice with ease.

For those who like to explore, I suggest you put your canoe in the river at the Antietam aqueduct and float downriver 3.5 miles to the sluice, located on the far right shore of the river, descending. You can hear "Houses" just around the bend as you make your approach. Tie everything in, then take the 150-foot sluice head-on and enjoy.

Shenandoah Falls and the Long Canal
The Potomac Company's "Long Canal" was located 5 miles below Houses Falls, along the bank of the Maryland side of the Potomac at the top of the present-day C & O Canal Dam No. 3 and a mile above the confluence of the Potomac and the Shenandoah rivers. The so-called Shenandoah Falls should not be confused with the many falls in the Shenandoah River. There is a natural ledge at the top of Shenandoah Falls that was sometimes exposed in low water by construction of a temporary 2-foot dam. This permitted boats to enter the public works canal race on the former Virginia side of the river.

The Potomac Company spent a considerable amount of money digging the Long Canal and armoring the river side of the canal with massive boulders that acted as revetment stones to protect the canal from the scouring effects of the river as it coursed along the outside edge (river's side of the canal). The Long Canal was 1 mile long

(1,760 yards), stretching from the top of Shenandoah Falls to the river confluences in the heart of Harpers Ferry Gap. The drop was 15 feet. At the head of the Long Canal, a rapid commenced. The bed of the river was uniformly covered with fixed rock to cut down on erosion.

Boats hugged the Maryland shore as they were slowly edged downward through the 1-mile walled sluiceway, a practice called "razing off." A lining path was cut slightly above the berm level on the east side of the through-channel to allow for the slow-rope descent of loaded boats or for hauling boats upstream on the return. The lining path can be seen today from the towpath below C & O Canal's Dam No. 3. The Long Canal was made up of three long partial channels, unjoined. The first channel had a fairly level bottom and a clear course about 18 to 20 feet wide. The other two sections had uneven bottoms and slightly irregular courses. Thus, the longboats survived the bypass around the falls with little or no damage to boats traveling in either direction.

The proposed route for what would be the future Chesapeake and Ohio Canal is shown on an 1825 survey map, published by the U.S. Army's Engineering Department and drawn by Lt. A. A. Wilson. The original is on file in the National Archives. At the time, the proposed C & O Canal was not formally named, but simply called "The Potomac Canal." The line of the existing 1-mile Long Canal is clearly shown on Lt. Wilson's map. The Long Canal adjoins the Maryland shoreline with its entrance route passing to the east of the small entrance island. It then curves right to begin the descent. This is probably the only drawing of the route of the Long Canal as it actually existed on its way downriver to join the confluences of the two great rivers at the base of Maryland Heights.

I recently examined a copy of Rembrandt Peale's 1814 painting of the Harpers Ferry Gap, the original of which is in the Walker Art Center Collection in Minneapolis. To my amazement, I could identify the precise outlet of the Long Canal on the Maryland side of the Potomac. The painting depicts two ferries crossing the confluence of the Potomac and Shenandoah rivers. The lower outlet of the Long Canal can be seen in the lower left quadrant of the painting in front of a large white building at the future location of Lock 33 on the C & O.

Several huge revetment rocks lining the river side of the Long Canal at this lower outlet can be discerned in the painting. In 1814, the Long Canal was in use, with 596 boats paying tolls to the Potomac Company that year.

Once the Potomac Company's longboats cleared the Long Canal they turned left, passed around the base of Maryland Heights, then proceeded through Harpers Ferry Gap. Next, they would clear Paynes Falls, then the Spout, and then make an easy run, 35 miles, to the top of the Seneca Falls bypass channel, at Seneca Breaks, the third great work of the Potomac Company, then to Great Falls, on to Little Falls, then to tidewater and the Georgetown wharves.

The Long Canal was obliterated when the C & O Canal Company built the C & O and its towpath on top of the old Long Canal route. The old revetment stones were rolled to their new location and used to construct the high one-mile towpath on the river side of the C & O Canal. I have spent many long hours at this location with the late geologist-engineer Bill Davies examining the terrain in the vicinity of the Long Canal hoping to find clues of its existence. As in the case of Houses Falls, I have yet to meet anyone who knows much about the primitive works of the Long Canal.

There are brief written descriptions of what Houses Falls and the Long Canal looked like, which can be found in the *Report of the Commissioners Appointed to Survey the River Potomac*, printed in 1823 by order of the Senate of the United States. This report is a rock-by-rock inspection trip on the river from the "Old Town Falls" to the lower end of Chapham's Island (which I believe to be above what is now Lower Mason Island). The inspection trip was conducted from August 8 to September 12, 1822. I doubt that the river has changed much between these locations since that time except for the high dams of the C & O Canal.

The commissioner's boat carried over 2,000 pounds of bureaucratic avoirdupois in the form of official representatives of the governor and council of Maryland. The commission's assignment was to expose the Potomac Company charter for not fulfilling the charter's provisions. One can tell, by savoring this amusing document, that the party was out of sorts and miserable in the August and September heat, and weary of continually running into shoals and scraping rocks for 31 days for a distance of some 140 wretched miles in the lowest of low August and September water conditions.

Even in freshets, boatmen must have preferred to carefully "line" their boats down the Long Canal rather than to lose control above the Gap. Once out of the Long Canal, at the speed the boats must have been going, it was essential that the boatmen had plenty of time to position the boats to take the Spout precisely head-on after they rounded the base of Maryland Heights.

The Spout

Washington had inspected the Spout as early as August 17, 1754, on his canoe trip from Patterson Creek to Harpers Ferry, and had erroneously considered it an impassable obstacle without a bypass. At first it was decided that a channel would have to be dug around the falls and one or two locks installed at an expense of £800, but none was ever built.

There are no clues to how the Spout received its contemporary name, White Horse. The name, perhaps, was assigned by canoeing groups drawing attention to the white plumes of spray at the bottom of the drop in high water. The designation Spout is well documented to before 1750, however, and is so written in Washington's diaries. White Horse is probably a post-World War II name.

The Potomac Company finally realized that despite its deep-throated roar and its menacing look, the Spout needed no special bypasses. It was found that on the return trips, even loaded boats could be laboriously pulled up the narrow chute with ropes or chains. Capstans, upright windlasses on which hauling ropes or chains were wound, were frequently used to pull boats up difficult falls or drops. No records identifying the location of capstans used in Potomac Company operations exist.

There are few reliable boat passages on the right side of the Potomac River (descending) after a boat leaves Harpers Ferry Gap due to the uneven corrugated rock patterns and souse holes. The natural opening at the Spout provided fast and "all or nothing" passage for the boatmen and, even today, it is a thrilling adrenaline-pumper.

If, in your investigations of Shenandoah Falls, you find heavy iron rings fastened to rocks at various locations, they were not put there for the Potomac Company boats to cling to. These rings were driven into the rock during the Civil War to tie or chain down military bridges. The Harpers Ferry park rangers have maps showing the locations of all the bridges and the sets of holding chains.

Seneca Falls Bypass

Seneca Falls Bypass is located 7 miles above Great Falls near the Virginia side of Seneca Falls. The Potomac Company bypass was 1,320 yards long and had an overall drop of 7 feet. The upriver end of the Seneca Bypass was built at a point slightly below the rubble dam built later by the C & O Canal Company on the Virginia bank 50 or more yards upstream of the old C & O Canal dam. Canoeists today take what is erroneously called "George Washington's Canal," which threads its way to join the historic bypass channel farther down Seneca Falls. When the Potomac Company was operating, a long wing dam at the top of Seneca Falls collected water from the river and directed it into the historic Seneca Bypass channel. The upper end of the wing dam was located in the center of the river. A large flat rock marks the old entrance to the authentic bypass channel and can still be seen.

Once you enter "George Washington's Canal," you descend into a labyrinth of braided channels, which periodically change locations in flood. Soon you will notice a wall constructed of thick flat stones placed on edge like shelves of leaning books. These and other startling discoveries await those who wish to explore this mile of channels and stonework. It is always cool in the Seneca Falls Bypass channel.

Great Falls Skirting Canal

The Great Falls Skirting Canal is located 7 miles above tidewater at the current site of Great Falls Park, Virginia, where the canal is preserved, but dry. This skirting canal circumnavigates the tumultuous barrage at Great Falls, providing the boatmen with a 77-foot drop through five lift locks. The remains of these locks can be seen today. A huge wing dam drew the boats from the river into the locks. There was an upper guard gate, a lower spillway, a collecting basin where boats could tie up, lower guard gates, and a lower (secondary) collecting basin.

Inside the Seneca Bypass. (Photo by Richard Stanton)

Great Falls. (Photo by Richard Stanton)

The small community of Matildaville was built along the skirting canal, providing housing and services for the canal workers and the boatmen who passed through on their way to and from Georgetown. The Revolutionary War hero, Richard Henry ("Light-Horse" Harry) Lee, founded the community, naming it for his first wife, Matilda. The little town grew with the Potomac Company, but vanished in 1830 when the company transferred its operations to the Maryland side of the river to begin towing canal boats up and down a watered canal with teams of mules. This project languished, and funds ran out. The State of Maryland was slow in putting up its promised share of money, and many stockholders were also delinquent. What funds there were, were spent at an alarming rate. In an economic move, the number of on-line managers was reduced. Even the £25 a year for contingency funds doled out to the officers of the company were eliminated. The project was to drag on for 16 more years before the first lock would be filled with water. This project was the final kiss of death for the old Potomac Company.

Ever since the Potomac Company was organized, Washington had

Approaching Potomac Company Lock 5, one of the
great engineering feats of the eighteenth century
blasted out of solid rock. (Photo by Richard
Stanton)

thoughts of withdrawing from the company, but his colleagues
would not hear of it. Washington longed for the quiet life at Mount
Vernon. Now, with the establishment of a constitutional form of government the call became clear, the beloved Washington was the unanimous choice to be the nation's chief executive. On the day of the Potomac Company's 1789 elections, Washington graciously permitted
his name to remain as president of the Potomac Company, and the
company's elections were conveniently postponed. With the post-
ponement of elections, the directors had to petition the Maryland

and Virginia legislatures to grant extension to the terms under the charter. This request was the first of ten additional amendatory acts between 1786 and 1820 to keep the Potomac Company operating under the terms of its original charter.

In spite of numerous difficulties, the Potomac Company completed the Great Falls Skirting Canal for a distance of 5,442 feet, along with a 1,200-foot wing dam. The remains of that dam can be seen today in low water. Next, a series of five stairway locks were constructed along the river for a mile or more. The first lock was 100 feet long and 14 feet wide. It would raise or lower boats 10 feet. Lock 2 was 100 feet long and 12 feet wide with a 16-foot lift. Locks 3, 4, and 5 were a series of three connected locks sharing common gates. A bend in Lock 3 allowed boats to turn 18 degrees. It had a lift of 14 feet. Locks 4 and 5 were blasted out of solid rock with black powder and were 100 feet long, 12 feet wide, and each lock a massive 18 feet deep, accounting for half the lift (38 feet) needed to skirt the 77-foot Great Falls drop.

Construction of the Great Falls canal system with its five locks was heralded in the American and European press, and was considered a remarkable feat of engineering, far ahead of its time. Never before had black powder been used as successfully, although there were some blasting accidents.

Washington knew every detail of construction work at Great Falls, visiting the site frequently, holding meetings, and conferring with workers on the progress of the project. Before the locks were completed, a series of inclined planes was erected to lower or raise cargoes. When the lock system was completed, use of these inclined planes was discontinued, and full lock operation began.

Washington did not live to see the completion of the Great Falls Bypass canal and locking system; nor was he permitted the great satisfaction of seeing his favorite internal improvement successfully launched. Washington had become so obsessed with anticipation and success for the project that guests at Mount Vernon remarked that the President spoke of little else. His frequent toasts, "Success to the navigation of the Potomac," were remembered by many visitors to Mount Vernon.

On December 13, 1799 the President became ill. The next day his

Grab ring downriver from Potomac Company Lock 5 that held chains or ropes to assist boatmen ascending the river to the outlet lock. (Photo by Richard Stanton)

condition worsened. The illness was diagnosed as "inflammatory quinsy." Washington died on December 14 at Mount Vernon at the age of 67. One of his great achievements lay less than 25 miles north of Mount Vernon at Great Falls, Virginia: tangible evidence of Washington's lifelong vision of a nation regionally linked by trade and commerce was being implemented.

The Little Falls Skirting Canal
The Little Falls Skirting Canal was 3,814 yards long (2.5 miles), with a drop of 37.5 feet. Constructed on the Maryland side of the river (left side, descending), it included three locks. Original locks were 100 feet long and 18 feet wide with an 11-foot lift. These were the first locks of their kind to be built in the United States. Potomac Company freight boats entered the Little Falls Bypass Canal above Little Falls, near the site of Lock 5 on the old C & O. The Little Falls tidewater outlet was located at Lock Cove near the present location of Fletcher's boathouse. The tidewater lock can be observed at this

location. The Little Falls Bypass was completed in 1795 allowing freight boats to use the inclined plane system at Great Falls seven years before the Great Falls locks were open to through-traffic in 1802. In 1818, new locks 12 feet wide and 100 feet long were built of stone in the same general area but at a different site. After leaving the tidewater lock, the Georgetown wharves were less than 4 miles ahead.

POTOMAC COMPANY COMMERCE

Although regulations required that each boat met minimum Potomac Company specifications, these rules were not rigidly enforced, in order not to make matters too expensive for the boat owners. All boats were numbered and licensed and very costly to build, usually requiring many years' savings for most boat owners. Owners such as the Hoblizel brothers of Cumberland owned more than one boat. They had several crews working on nearby farms ready to move down the river at a moment's notice during the spring freshet season. The crew loaded the boat as the water went up. Lost cargoes, equipment, and sometimes even a lost boat were not uncommon. Crew members could drown. Cargoes were laboriously carried around huge fallen trees and other impediments, then reloaded again with great losses in time and energy. Steersmen were heroes of sorts, not unlike race car drivers of today. Individual steersmen had their loyal following, and bets were made on the nearest times of arrival both at the Georgetown wharves and at the Cumberland end. Steersmen were prima donnas, but they could not afford to choose vanity over cargo safety and the lives of their companions.

Running a 2-ton boat with a 10-ton cargo around wing dams and through sluices with only a foot of water underneath the keel was unthinkable from the boat owner's view. Even though boatmen were for the most part highly skilled navigators, a 75-foot boat moving in high water would navigate more safely with cargoes and crew than one threading its way with a foot of water under its keel. It was the hope of the Potomac Company, in the beginning, that boats would run in both directions in low and high water conditions. This was understandable in theory, but was impractical. Starting a run down the river with a heavy cargo and only 1 foot of water underneath could, with lowering levels, bring the boat to a sudden stop in the middle of the river, one of the boatman's biggest nightmares. The company made many errors, but attempted to correct them as time went along. Potomac Company financial losses were largely attributed to the fact that boat owners were either unable or unwilling to carry freight on the river more than 45 days a year, subject to the whims of the river.

In the end, it was unlikely that investors would have financed these ventures without some daring concepts being offered, such as blasting rocks and going through locks and working sluiceways. These were just a few of the modern touches that prompted investors to part with their money. The lessons learned on the Virginia side of Great Falls served as the great precursor for the success of the lock systems on the Chesapeake and Ohio Canal, to be constructed at a later date, across the river on the Maryland side.

Wing dams, which reached out into the swift water to better confine the river's flow, were built to divert water flow toward works requiring great quantities of water for navigation. Large works were located just above Great Falls. These were needed to insure that freight boats could enter the approaches to Great Falls satisfactorily as the river widens at this point. To make the journey upstream from below the falls, iron rings were attached to stanchions and were driven into the faces of huge rocks lying along the shoreline on the upriver approach to the Great Falls Bypass. Long chains or ropes were secured to the rings and were used by the boatmen on their way upstream to better gain purchase as they laboriously inched their way to reach Lock No. 5, the outlet lock. The locking system was reversed and the boatmen, upon reaching the lower lock, then raised their boat upwards 77 feet through all five locks to the top of the locking system. From here the boatmen could continue their journey upstream.

With longboats up to 75 and 80 feet in length, sharp turns were difficult and frequently calamitous in any depth of water. The most dangerous set of turns, always worrisome, were the two at Difficult Run Rapids, 1.5 miles below Great Falls. A heavy, unstable freight boat entering the turns first had to clear clusters of rocks just before

Below Great Falls. Difficult Run, near the center of the photograph, got its name from the Potomac Company boatmen who found it difficult to make turns at this location. (Photo by Abbie Rowe, courtesy of the National Park Service)

an elbow turn at the bottom of Difficult Run Rapid. The swift prevailing currents there tended to pull boats into the rocks on the left and shoal water on the right. Once cleared, the boat had to be positioned for a sweeping left turn. As the boats entered the elbow, they tended to yaw toward the base of the unyielding rocks below what is now the Madeira School property, with frequently disastrous consequences.

There is no record of how fast a 2-ton freight boat with cargo would clip by this turn of turns. It is well known that Difficult Run was so-named during the Potomac Company days because of the turning difficulties at its mouth, coupled with the mix of cross-currents above and at the run, at different water levels. It was not unusual for the boatmen to accommodate the river when walls and sluices gave way or when rocks shifted as the boats yawed into rocks along the shoals, a common occurrence.

Some boats carried as much as 15 tons of cargo and drew 18 inches of water, loaded. It was the skill and experience of the steersmen that kept boats on course. The rest of the crew kept the boat away from the most dangerous rocks and shoals. Trying to recover a 10- to 15-ton cargo from an overturned freight boat could take many hours or even days in troubled high water conditions. Frequently the full cargo washed out into the river, particularly if the cargo faced upriver after the upset. Ropes were fragile and parted easily. Whiskey and flour barrels leaked badly when stressed.

Some so-called boats were nothing more than log rafts, called arks, on which lumber or farm produce would be tied and floated downriver. Upon reaching Georgetown, a raft would be broken up and the logs sold for the best price. Often the boatmen then walked back to their point of origin, sometimes traveling 30 miles per day over trails along the river. Freight boats 50-feet long or under were sometimes called bateaux, an indication of the French influence, which came from the most southern U.S. freight-boat cultures.

Boats called Potomac River "sharpers" were usually pointed at each end with part of their decks covered with tarpaulins stretched over hoops, resembling Conestoga wagons. Illogically, "sharpers" were not named for their sharp ends. In Colonial days, rapids were referred to as "sharp water," hence any boat used to ply "sharp water" was a sharper, pointed ends or not.

The trip to Georgetown and return required only a few pounds of bacon, bread, and two or three small barrels of whiskey for the crew. Wild game and an abundant supply of fish from the river helped provide sustenance. Six crew members were common, which included a head oarsman, usually the captain, a steersman, and enough polemen at each side of the boat to push the boat away from dangerous rocks and other impediments. Downriver stops were avoided, as boatmen were anxious to be the first to reach the Georgetown wharves in order to get the highest possible prices for their cargoes. Boatmen camped out on the decks of their boats and built cooking fires on the tops of large flat stones placed on the floor planks at the bottoms of their boats.

The boats carried diverse loads that included whiskey, potash, bar and pig iron, hogshead staves, tobacco, linseed, hides, hemp, beef,

Eighteenth-century replica river freight boat *Minnie Lee* entering the Seneca Bypass Canal above Great Falls. (Photo by Kenneth Garrett)

Minnie Lee layover at Fifteenmile Creek. (Photo by Richard L. Stanton)

For the Potomac riverphile, there could be no greater thrill than the launching of the replica late eighteenth-century river boat, *Minnie Lee*, at Cumberland on April 30, 1987. It was brought from the James River to the Potomac by Joe Ayers, then president of the Virginia Canals and Navigations Society. Joe is from Columbia, Virginia. He brought the boat to the Potomac to celebrate the Bicentennial of the United States Constitution. The *Minnie Lee* is 49 feet long and 7 feet wide, weighing in at 2 tons without cargo. Ayers's boat was designed and built after an authentic freight "bateau" used on the James River. The Archeological Society of Virginia was the principal partner in the exhumation of that bateau from the Richmond Canal Basin with assistance from the members of the James River Navigation Company, Inc. Boats like this were common throughout the southeastern United States from 1782 to 1817. Most of the freight boats used in the Potomac River freight trade were usually 60 to 75 feet long, but there is no doubt that Ayers's replica boat fits right into the Potomac Company era because lengths, widths, and designs varied.

The only near-find of a Potomac River boat of commerce has been identified by noted naval historian Dr. Norman N. Rubin. It was a dugout canoe found buried in the mud along the South Branch of the Potomac River. Dr. Rubin feels that the boat was probably built by a slave on a plantation bordering the Potomac. The dugout follows an African model. One possible model would be a dugout from Lake Byunyoni similar to those fashioned by the Banyankole people of Uganda. The narrow boat has a classic pronounced sheer at its bow and stern and a graceful line. It was cut from a single poplar log, 31 inches in diameter. The boat was built before the Potomac Company started operation, and could date as early as 1775. The hull lines are utilitarian. The plan for the boat must certainly have come from recollections of one made in Africa, or of one made in this country by someone skilled in African boatmaking techniques. The dugout is 28 feet long and can be paddled or poled. It is 18 inches wide at the stern and 26 inches amidships. The dugout is typical of many such boats that moved from farm to farm, along the shores of the Potomac, trading produce or other goods. It is displayed at Great Falls Park, Virginia, at the visitor's center, and is well worth seeing. Both the dugout and the prototype for the *Minnie Lee* owe their long existence to the unique properties of river-bottom mud, which acted as a preservative over the years.

The Potomac River has its unique peculiarities and requirements, just as other rivers have theirs. Rivers, as the first successful and practical means of transportation to and from the frontiers of the new nation, required different types of boats depending on a variety of factors. Shenandoah River boats operated in less turbulent waters and the trade was brisk. Susquehanna boats had running boards outside their hulls, allowing polers to walk without impediment outside the boat while they poled. Durham boats, also known as Schenectady boats, were some 60 feet long and carried a mast set in the foredeck used for running with the wind and, according to the New York State Museum, operated in the Mohawk River, Lake Ontario, and along the St. Lawrence River until 1780. Potomac boatmen had boards inside the hulls to avoid hanging up on rocks, a problem not often encountered on other rivers. Potomac boats had open decks and canvas coverings much like those on Conestoga wagons.

Joe was blessed. Potomac water levels in 1987 on April 30 were high and clear, ideal for his James River bateau. Joe and his crew stopped along the way as they proceeded downriver. They would pull the skiff to shore each afternoon and set up camp, right on the boat. *Minnie Lee* is handsome; it is named after a Fluvanna County, Virginia, historian. Joe also has a second boat, the *Columbia.* During the trip downriver from Cumberland, Maryland, weekend rains raised the river more than 3 feet. This medium-high level lasted all the way to Great Falls. *Minnie Lee* made 3 miles an hour from Little Orleans (Fifteenmile Creek) to Hancock, against fierce winds. Boats like *Minnie Lee* are made to float rather than be propelled. Traditionally, each boat had a steersman, usually two and sometimes three side polemen, and a head oarsman, who might also be the captain; he stood in the front of the boat pushing the bow to either side to avoid dangerous rocks.

Joe and his crew enjoyed themselves, and folks from near and far met the boat as the boat's schedule was published. Fascinated visitors brought many country meals, pies, and homemade breads. Each night saw a host of victuals fit for King Joe and his royal crew. In addition to Ayers, Warren O'Brien, a poleman who donated the lumber to build *Minnie Lee,* and Paul Parrish, Joe's brother-in-law from Richmond was also on board. Paul helped Joe build *Minnie Lee* and acted as the stern sweep man. Dave Brown and Craig Foutz made up the balance of the crew. The crew did their own cooking and took care of the on-board housekeeping. Following tradition, flat stones were laid in the bottom of the boat to accommodate small cooking fires. Each night after dinner, Joe Ayers would bring out his four-string banjo made from a gourd, the type used long ago on the rivers of America.

I was fortunate, as superintendent of the C & O Canal Park at the time, to have followed the saga of Joe Ayers's *Minnie Lee* from Cumberland to Great Falls. I stopped by now and then to say "hello" in the evening when the boat was tied to shore.

The real test came when Joe and his crew arrived at Shenandoah Falls (in the Potomac) at the top of C & O Canal's Dam No. 3, above Harpers Ferry. I would really see a reenactment of an authentic eighteenth-century river boat doing a free-fall down Shenandoah Falls. No more guessing, no more theories. The huge 2-ton boat looked cumbersome and unwieldy but it glided smoothly, keeping up with the current. When it hit a medium-sized rock, it rode right over, then slid back on course with a minimum of damage, thanks to its heavy weight and its nonchalant manner in dealing with these crises.

Joe scouted Shenandoah Falls with me a few days before he ran them in *Minnie Lee.* Having raced through these falls many times in a canoe, I urged Joe to run the Maryland side (the Needles), but he had to make a sharp right turn just before reaching Harpers Ferry in order to reach his riverside campsite just above the confluence of the Potomac and the Shenandoah. The water was up and he wanted to try the falls right of center so he could make the right turn into the mouth of the Shenandoah at the completion of the run. In normal to low water, turns are tricky here because of limestone ridges that cross the river at right angles to the river's flow.

On the appointed day, Joe positioned the bow exactly where he wanted it. Suddenly, he dropped down the falls, dodging rocks and weaving the boat through roaring rapids. Next, he maneuvered the boat into a sharp right elbow turn at the confluence into Harpers Ferry beach where he arrived wet but right side up, pleased and triumphant.

Joe is one of the best boat handlers I have seen, and I especially admired his skills on this trip. Where Joe comes from, a lot of folks make authentic replicas of James River boats. They race and go on camping trips, and enjoy just being James River boatmen from the

past. Families frequently join in the fun and do their share of the hard work. I must admit, having Joe around for two weeks was thrilling.

On May 11, Joe's boat pushed into the Shenandoah and headed across the Potomac to the left margin (descending) to dare run the fall of falls, the Spout (White Horse Rapid). Once positioned above the Spout it would be a simple shot out of the cannon, straight ahead to the chute and then one short lurch and down. It is only a 15-foot drop, but it is sinister looking, and the deep, threatening roar never stops. There is a "keeper" rock on the bottom, at the left, known as a widow-maker. I had no doubt in my mind, watching Joe, that the 80-foot boats of old would have navigated the Spout exquisitely. Had the Potomac Company built a bypass channel here as originally planned, there probably would have been many rollovers caused by the swift water and the cumbersome positioning that would have been required to accommodate the bypass.

Joe's crew did what the Potomac Company boatmen surely must have done as they approached the Spout: held on for dear life! Unbelievably, crew member Dave Brown took photographs as they dropped down into the bottom of the Spout's saddle. A broadside into one of the many rocks in the vicinity would have meant "Good Bye, *Minnie*," but Joe's style was at its best that day.

Once through the Spout, Minnie Lee moved quickly. Joe and his crew were soon through Paynes Falls, with Maryland Heights towering behind them. Four days later, Joe Ayers skillfully eased Minnie Lee right above the wing dam at the entrance to the Great Falls Bypass Canal, which hadn't been used by a longboat for 160 years.

----

pork, flax, coal, and varied assortments of farm produce in season. Tobacco was a preferred cargo. The difference in the value of bringing tobacco to market rather than wheat was two to one in favor of tobacco; however, tobacco prices fluctuated, sometimes wildly. Plentiful supplies of tobacco were grown in the fields around Georgetown and in the northern neck of Virginia. Mountain and valley tobacco was not preferred over the product grown in the lower reaches of the river. Tobacco flavor is greatly influenced by the soil in which it is grown. Shallow mountainous lands upriver did not produce favored plants for general consumption or trans-shipment to Europe. Barreled whiskey made a lucrative cargo compared to just hauling raw grain, and could earn a three to one ratio. Whiskey was a fragile cargo, however, heavy to handle and nearly always subject to total loss in the event of a river upset.

On the return trip upriver, boats often carried sugar, wine, English cloth, and sought-after manufactured items. Valuable upriver cargoes were loaded on the boats and forced upriver with great difficulty by push poles, sweep oars, or by laborious hauling by rope or chain. Many a mountain housewife yearned for pots and pans and decorated china from Europe. These kinds of cargoes were sold quickly upriver and brought enormous profits. When trading at the Georgetown wharves went well, it was not unusual for a boat owner to make as much profit on a return trip as on the initial downriver run. Cargoes rode safer on slow upriver hauls despite the wracking labor required. When the boats arrived in Cumberland they were often decorated with green boughs and met at the landings at Water Street, at the old City Water Works, or below Cumberland Falls.

Tolls were collected at various points by agents of the Potomac Company, usually at river confluences. Tolls could be paid with any kind of foreign coin, the value of which never stopped fluctuating. There was no national currency at the time, and the payment of tolls seemingly was a matter of utter confusion. But the boatmen generally paid their tolls. In the event tolls were not paid, the vessel and its cargo were seized and sold at auction. In addition, a fine was levied. This iron-handed treatment assured payment, on the spot. Tolls for a through-trip to Georgetown ranged from the equivalent of $10 to $12 for the largest cargoes, subject to the kinds of goods carried and final destinations.

A freight boat could carry as many as 150 barrels of flour on each trip, a load weighing as much as 10 to 15 tons. During the freshet season, boatmen waited impatiently for weeks for the river to rise. Boats were usually loaded and ready to leave their home ports with little or no notice. Boatmen were employed as farm hands or at other unskilled jobs between downriver runs, but their mettle had been tested at the poles and all were generally highly skilled river runners.

All eyes were on the river; when it finally rose to the desired level, experienced boatmen appeared from nowhere, eager to guide the run to the Georgetown wharves while others loaded the boats with supplies for the trip. When all was ready, the 197-mile river race from Cumberland began. As the river rose from its banks, the boats were released into the fast currents. Families, as well as the curious, were at the riverbank to see the boats off, often weeping and praying for the safe return of the boatmen.

Boatmen could earn far more on the sharpers than they could in the fields at home. Many boat owners, especially those who owned several boats with prized steersmen standing by, earned enormous profits from these dangerous enterprises, as did the boat handlers. In its best year, 1811, 1,300 boats paid tolls to the Potomac Company. During the 23 years of the Potomac Company, 14,000 boats carried cargoes down the river to tidewater with an estimated cargo value of near $10 million.

Boat owners could lose everything on a run or turn a good profit, depending on the moods of the freshets. Floods and freshets provided the only reliable navigation for some 30 to 45 days per year. The wildness of the currents and the suddenness of its courses and meanders frequently produced huge rock fragments and loose stones, which often rose up over the entire bed of the river, leaving little or no passage for boats. Such situations required the utmost exertion of strength and agility on the part of the crews. As a consequence of the unpredictability of the water levels required for navigation, farmers, millers, and merchants frequently faced financial ruin. Sometimes a deceitful small rise in the water levels induced boat crews to proceed downriver where, after 40 miles, low water levels compelled boatmen to stop before cargoes were damaged or lost.

Conversely, when the rains came too soon, there were no crops or goods ready for transport. Perfect levels could also be disastrous, forcing all goods on the market at one time, resulting in low profits and the sacrifices of the year's labor. Boat owners sometimes entered into contracts to deliver certain cargoes to the wharves within deadlines. No stone was left unturned to squeeze a shred of profit from these daring and speculative freight hauls, so delicate was the balance between profits and losses.

A letter dated December 20, 1822, from the Potomac Company to

Entries from Table Compiled by J. Moore, Jr., Treasurer of Potomac Company (Senate Document No. 29, January 27, 1823, Paper B)

Year	Boats	Tonnage	Tolls Received	Total Est. Value
1800	296	1,643	$2,138.58	$129,414.00
1801	413	2,993	4,210.19	328,445.32
1802	305	1,952	3,479.69	163,916.00
1803	493	5,549	9,353.93	345,472.82
1804	426	3,823	7,765.58	284,040.60
1805	405	3,208	5,213.24	340,334.18
1806	203	1,226	2,123.69	86,790.40
1807	573	8,155	15,080.42	551,896.47
1808	508	5,994	9,924.27	337,007.47
1809	603	6,767	9,094.80	365,628.00
1810	568	5,374	7,915.85	318,237.62
1811	1,300	16,350	22,542.89	925,074.80
1812	613	9,214	11,471.37	515,525.75
1813	623	7,916	11,816.22	423,340.32
1814	596	5,987	9,109.82	312,093.72
1815	613	6,354	9,789.57	489,498.15
1816	550	6,132	7,501.52	357,661.00
1817	856	8,197	13,948.23	787,994.00
1818	746	9,778	10,332.26	781,924.00
1819	775	7,550	12,514.04	565,010.62 ½
1820	917	16,506	13,107.31 ½	420,818.15
1821	760	11,400	12,490.61	318,810.00
1822	782	11,730	11,103.50 ½	369,522.62
Totals	13,924	162,798	$221,927.67	$9,357,456.76 ½

His Excellency the Governor of Maryland, included a table showing the numbers of boats, the tonnage, total tolls collected, and the estimated value of freight hauled in each year, from August 1, 1799, to August 1, 1822.

Of the entire sum collected for tolls, only one dividend was ever paid to the stockholders. In 1802, a dividend of $3,890.00 was paid. This, with $1,088.07 in hand subtracted, shows the remainder, $216,949.60, as the amount spent on the operation and works of the company.

Chapter 5.

RACE FOR THE OHIO: THE ESTABLISHMENT OF THE CHESAPEAKE AND OHIO CANAL COMPANY

By 1825, the Erie Canal had been completed, linking the Hudson River with Lake Erie. New York held new-found dominance in the western trade. It was the success of the Erie Canal that finally brought down the proprietors of the Potomac Company. The "improvement" of the navigation of the Potomac River from tidewater to the highest point practicable and the portage to the waters of the Ohio still seemed as elusive as ever. Thus, after 36 years and an expenditure of $729,380, the proprietors agreed to permit a commission comprised of members of the legislatures of Virginia and Maryland to look into the affairs of the Potomac Company, to examine the state of the navigation of the river, and to report on whether the provisions of the charter had been met. The commissioners concluded that the company had not complied with the terms and conditions of their incorporation. The company had expended their capital stock and had incurred an enormous debt. Moreover, navigation could only be conducted on the river for some 45 days a year.

Subsequently, the proprietors of the Potomac Company agreed to give up their charter. Despite the frustrating years during the construction of the Potomac Company's river works, there were still believers in the Potomac River as a navigational route that were willing to try all over again, this time on the Maryland side of the river with a watered canal, a towpath, locks, and mules. In this way the Chesapeake and Ohio Canal Company came into being with new hopes and dreams, not unlike those of George Washington and his original directors on that grand and happy day, May 17, 1785, in Alexandria.

In 1828, the Potomac Company's charter was transferred across the river from Virginia to the Maryland side where a watered canal could be built from the mouth of Rock Creek, below Georgetown, upriver, over mountains, to the waters of the Ohio. The proposition was that canal boats could be pulled by mules in either direction. The major tonnage would be brought from the Ohio territories, and would include all manner of furs and "big-vein" coal from the Georges Creek coal fields. The watered canal would have enough lift locks to raise it from near sea level at Georgetown to a mountain elevation of 1,900 feet above sea level at the canal's summit. Uniformly sized boats (not barges) would fit uniformly sized locks. It was proposed that great dams and lakes in the high Alleghenies would furnish water for the canal's locks. Great aqueducts would carry canal water over the tributaries emptying into the Potomac and Ohio river watersheds.

With the transfer of the Potomac Company Charter and all assets, the Chesapeake and Ohio Canal Company was entitled to all rights and privileges originally granted to the Potomac Company under its charter in 1784. The act to incorporate the Chesapeake and Ohio Canal Company was passed by the Legislature of Virginia on January 27, 1824. The State of Maryland, by an act of its legislature passed on January 31, 1825, confirmed the Virginia act as did the Congress of the United States on March 3, 1825. On May 16, 1825, the full and unqualified assent of the Potomac Company was declared and signified by corporate act. The Chesapeake and Ohio Canal Company accepted the surrender and conveyance of the Potomac Company's charter and all assets on September 17, 1828.

Charles F. Mercer of Virginia was an obvious choice to serve as the first president of the Chesapeake and Ohio Canal Company. Mercer was the chairman of the Committee on Roads and Canals of the House of Representatives, and had in hand over $3.5 million of federal money with which to begin construction. It was planned that the canal would leap to Pittsburgh to capture the Ohio trade and direct it down the Potomac River to Georgetown.

An auspicious ceremony was planned for July 4, 1828 at the head of Little Falls, along the Potomac River above Georgetown, to commemorate the formation of the Chesapeake and Ohio Canal Company. President John Quincy Adams raised the first spadeful of dirt, symbolizing the start of the canal's construction. Washington City was alive with people that morning. At Tilley's Hotel, the directors of the canal company played host to their distinguished guests, including President Adams and his cabinet, many distinguished ambassadors and ministers of foreign countries, survivors of the Revolution, and other dignitaries. With the President leading the procession, the crowds marched to the river to the accompaniment of the Marine band, embarking on the stout little steamboat, the *Surprise.*

Surprise made its way upriver to the river outlet lock at the downriver end of the Little Falls Bypass Canal, 2 miles below Little Falls. The group prepared to board old and decaying Potomac Company longboats that were barely floating in the unused lock. The boats were pulled upstream for 2 miles where the ceremony was held. The city newspaper, the *National Intelligencer,* reported:

Disembarking, the company marched to the canal boats [Potomac Company longboats] lying in the old canal built by the labors of George Washington's Potomac Company nearly fifty years before. The delightful music gave place to the salutes of the riflemen as the President arrived on the ground. The party formed a hollow square about the spot of ground chosen for the raising of the first spadeful of earth. Then, midst silence so intense as to chasten the animation of hope and to hallow the enthusiasm of joy, the Mayor of Georgetown with appropriate remarks, handed to Mr. Mercer, President of the Canal Company, the implement with which the ground was to be broken. After he had concluded his remarks he handed the spade to the President [Adams] who made the address, after which he attempted to sink the spade in the soil at the designated spot. The spade hit a large stump under the surface of the soil. After repeating the stroke three or four times without success, President Adams threw off his coat and, at last, raised a spadeful of earth, after which cheers burst forth from the crowd.

On the same day, another important inaugural ceremony was being conducted at James Carroll's Mount Clair estate, west of the city of

Baltimore. The illustrious 90-year-old Charles Carroll of Carrollton, the last surviving signer of the Declaration of Independence, laid the cornerstone for the Baltimore and Ohio Railroad, which was planned to reach the Ohio River at Wheeling, West Virginia, and continue beyond.

The concern of the citizens of Baltimore was that with the Chesapeake and Ohio Canal terminating at Georgetown, the profitable western trade would bypass their city. A railroad system might be the answer. In these early days, railroads, at best, were experimental. The Liverpool and Manchester Railroad in England got off to a shaky beginning in 1825. Its success was uncertain, but there were those in Baltimore who had an unshakable faith in the future of railroads. Subsequently, a distinguished committee of citizens, including Philip E. Thomas, Benjamin C. Howard, George Brown, and other men of note in the Baltimore business community, recommended that a double-track railroad be built between Baltimore and the Ohio River. With the railroad fever warming, the Maryland legislature, on February 28, 1827, eagerly approved an act authorizing the issuance of a charter that was quickly confirmed by Virginia and, a year later, by Pennsylvania.

Despite this legislative support, railroads had hardly gone beyond the horsecar stage. There were only two railroads in operation in the country at the time, one small freight line in Quincy, Massachusetts, and a coal mining railroad in Mauch Chunk, Pennsylvania, which operated a distance of only 12 miles at a maximum speed of 12 miles an hour. Steam was being tried in England with some success. It wouldn't be long before Peter Cooper of New York would journey to Baltimore to build a small locomotive, the *Tom Thumb*. Cooper's little engine made its first run from Baltimore to Ellicotts Mills on August 30, 1830, pulling a car full of passengers, the first passenger journey by steam locomotive ever made in America.

Meanwhile, the proposal to successfully dig a ditch wide and deep enough to carry canal boats 341 miles up, down, and around mountains with elevations up to 1,900 feet, through 398 locks, and a 4-mile-long tunnel, at a cost of $22 million, seemed, to many, to be the height of folly. Yet there were many who were convinced it could be done, despite the use of primitive tools and the limitations of engineering knowledge at the time.

After the ceremonies of July 4, 1828, dirt continued to fly and track-laying began in earnest. Both projects were headed West and each party was determined to grab the lion's share of the Georges Creek coal commerce along the Potomac's North Branch and to be the first to reach both the eastern and western markets. The race was on. Despite the pitched battle that ensued, there was one thing for sure, with the advent of the canal and the railroad, the towns and valleys along the Potomac would never be the same.

Both the canal company and the railroad were engrossed in determining their precise routes west. The canal company, faced with the necessity to draw upon the Potomac River for its lifeblood, chose the route surveyed by the U.S. Engineers and Geddes and Roberts, which virtually held to the river's edge most of the distance to Cumberland. The route west to Cumberland was obvious, but above the confluence of the Potomac and Wills Creek, the route to Pittsburgh remained purposefully vague to avoid land speculation and its devastating artificial rises in land values.

Construction of the central or mountain division of the canal west of Cumberland certainly was the most difficult and expensive. Three general routes from Cumberland to Pittsburgh were under consideration. All had merit but no final decisions had been made. The first route was from Cumberland by way of Wills Creek and the Casselman River to the confluence of Turkeyfoot, Pennsylvania. The second, from Cumberland, followed the North Branch of the Potomac to a point below its headwaters at Fairfax Stone, then across nearby Backbone Mountain to the Cheat River. This plan contemplated a portage road from the Potomac's highest point of navigation to the Cheat River, then north to the Monongahela River and on to Pittsburgh. This was the route always favored by George Washington. Off-loading cargoes into wagons and then reloading to boats made sense rather than spending valuable time and construction money for long tunnels at the summit level.

The third route under consideration, and most favored by the engineers, known as the Garrett County route, was the passage from

Cumberland, following the North Branch of the Potomac, proceeding upstream to the mouth of the Savage River; up the Savage and then by way of Crabtree Creek, then by a tunnel through Little Backbone Mountain to the waters of the Youghiogheny, then to Pittsburgh.

Concurrently, Deep Creek was examined as a possible alternate route for the continuation of the canal to Pittsburgh. A narrow pass in a ridge of the glades, through which Deep Creek made its way, was considered for placemnt of a dam 20 feet high and 40 or 50 yards long. Thus, the meadows could be inundated and an immense pond formed equal to 3 or 4 miles in length and as much as half a mile wide. This reservoir, it was believed, would furnish sufficient water for a canal if carried through a dividing ridge to a 2-mile tunnel, providing the means to descend and ascend both sides of the mountains to the Monongahela on the west and to Savage River on the east.

Early in 1824, Congress appropriated $80,000 for surveys and plans for construction of canals. Captain McNeil, assisted by seven army engineers, and Captain Shriver with three civil engineers, were appointed to select and survey a canal route above the mountains. The route favored by the engineers followed the Savage River and Crabtree Run, then by two cuts and a tunnel of 1 mile, 688 yards, through Little Backbone Mountain to Deep Creek, then by Deep Creek and Buffalo Marsh Run; then through-cuts and a 2-mile tunnel to the waters of Bear Creek; then down Bear Creek to its junction with the Youghiogheny. From the mouth of Savage River to the mouth of Bear Creek by canal would be 41 miles. This plan provided for a 23-foot storage dam at the head of the rapids of Deep Creek, to flood an area of 948,924 square yards with a capacity of 2,214,156 cubic yards, to raise and lower canal boats through a series of locks. The lift or "rise" from the mouth of the Savage River to the "base mark" on Deep Creek bridge was 1,432 feet.

The mountain section of the C & O Canal was never built. It was agreed, even at this early date, that transportation by railroad might prove to be more practical in the long run. Had the summit level been pierced for the canal, there is no doubt the route through the

Deep Creek glades would have been the unanimous choice with its natural water systems beckoning at the summit.

The general map and its reduction that were prepared by the Topographic Bureau of the Army Engineering Department, under Lt. Colonel J. J. Abert, were masterful for their time, especially the maps accompanying the *Report Upon the Contemplated Canal,* drawn by Lt. J. D. Findlay, of October 1826. The scale and delineation of these maps are remarkably accurate.

Meanwhile, the route for the B & O Railroad was finally agreed upon. It would follow the Patapsco River Valley, then the Monocacy River Basin to the Potomac, then up the Potomac Valley. It was always proposed that the railroad would also follow the Potomac River on the Maryland side. All seemed well until the rival enterprises reached Point of Rocks, 12 miles below Harpers Ferry on the Maryland side of the river. Point of Rocks was so named because of the natural cleft in the Catoctin Mountains at this location caused by millions of years of head-on scouring by the Potomac River. As the Potomac turns upriver, virtually no shelf exists on the Maryland side leaving precious little room for a canal, much less an additional right-of-way for a two-track railroad. Point of Rocks would be an ideal place for the railroad to test the strength of the canal company's "prior rights of location," thought to have been conveyed under the original Potomac Company Charter. If the railroad and the canal company were vying for the same piece of property, either by direct purchase or condemnation, the canal company, by virtue of its prior rights, inherited under the Potomac Company Charter, would prevail if all went well in the courts. The canal company secured an injunction prohibiting the railroad from continuing farther up the valley. The railroad secured three injunctions in response. The railroad could afford to wait for a decision as it would soon be doing business in Baltimore and Frederick and preparing to move people and freight to and from Virginia and Maryland to points east and west. The advantage of the railroad was its ability to engage in business almost the moment tracks were laid, whereas the canal would lie dry until it was able to reach its next water source. The devastating time delays at Point of Rocks threatened to eclipse the canal for good. Without its legal right of prior location, the railroad could push the canal so far inland that its water flows and critical elevations could be seriously compromised. The matter was purely political, with Baltimore's influence seeing to it that the state would not intervene, thereby assuring a costly and continuing mutual procrastination.

Finally, in January 1832, the Court of Appeals of Maryland upheld the canal company's chartered right of prior location. Both parties lost financially and also lost valuable time, for while the railroad was fiddling, its advantage in time was burning up, too, with Philadelphia and New York steadily increasing their positions in the eternal search for the western trade during those critical four years. The railroad was allowed one track around Point of Rocks and, thereafter, was required to move its works to the Virginia side of the river. There were no winners.

The canal company now prepared to move forward to make up for lost time. Almost at once a disastrous epidemic of Asiatic cholera struck, scattering workers and contractors into the surrounding countryside. With the rampant contagion about, it was almost impossible to find workers willing even to bury the dead.

High land prices and a precarious financial position added to the canal's problems. Having already spent $7 million on the canal, Maryland was once again beseeched to come to the aid of the canal company by agreeing to a preferred pledge of the canal's future income. A mortgage was approved just in time.

With new financial means, the canal prepared to break loose at Dam No. 6 and move up the line and try to reach Cumberland, 50 miles upriver. In March and July 1846, two devastating freshets inflicted great damage on canal works along the entire line, including the loss of 80 feet of Dam No. 4, which was carried away by the swollen Potomac River. Matters were corrected and soon work above Dam No. 6 continued. In October 1847 the canal braced itself for a major flood. Its high water marks surpassed all previous levels. Additional freshets in November and December continued to keep canal operations at a standstill. Operations at Dam No. 6 were not resumed until February 1848. In all, over $48,000 was spent to put the canal back to its condition before the floods.

Not even the most optimistic would have believed that within a few years after the settlement of the Point of Rocks disruptions the state of railroad engineering art would have accelerated to the extent it did. Until 1834, the *York*, the *Atlantic*, and the *Franklin* were the only locomotives on the rail line. By the end of the year more locomotives were added and the era of horse-drawn cars was coming to a close. The railroad forged ahead and despite unending financial crises and the continuing cries for more investment capital, the B & O Railroad reached Cumberland at the end of 1842. Almost without pause, the B & O Railroad headed for Wheeling and the Ohio River. The C & O Canal was years behind schedule. Cumberland, and now Wheeling, would be no more than stops along the way as the B & O stayed right on the heels of the Pennsylvania Railroad determined to reach the Ohio River first. The B & O's race with the canal company to reach the Ohio had been won, but the triumph was meaningless. Not only was the B & O moving as fast as it could to reach Wheeling, it was increasing its traffic to and from the Georges Creek coal fields. It seemed unlikely that the canal would ever go beyond Cumberland and even now the canal, plagued with its worst financial difficulties encountered so far, began to talk of discontinuing construction at Dam No. 6 and making Dam No. 6 the head of canal navigation. All the while the B & O was transporting coal from Georges Creek to the then Virginia side of the river at Dam No. 6 to be hauled by canal boats to Georgetown. Huge iron rings, used to tie canal boats to the river's edge while coal was being loaded, can still be seen at the head of Dam No. 6 on the West Virginia side of the river. They are embedded in the fallen capstones that once rested on the top of the walls along the south side of the dam pool.

Finally, on October 10, 1850, the C & O Canal opened for business along its entire 184½-mile length. The *Daily National Intelligencer* in Washington described a procession of canal boats, led by the excursion packet *Jenny Lind*. The canal boat *C. B. Fisk*, loaded with Georges Creek coal, headed down-canal for the port of Georgetown, symbolically opening the waterway for business. The events of the day closed with a supper and ball in the evening given by citizens at Cumberland's Heflefinger's Hotel.

Two years later the B & O Railroad reached the Ohio River at

Wheeling, Virginia (West Virginia), but the Pennsylvania Railroad had reached the river first. The number of railroads seeking routes to the West grew, as did the aggressive competition, leaving the B & O little time or inclination to be concerned about canal matters in Cumberland, the Queen City. With the continuing advances in railroad technology and the building of heavier and faster engines, the era of fragile and unpredictable water-filled ditches seemed almost over, yet the C & O Canal, despite continual floods, precarious financial problems, and costly labor unrest, would, somehow, continue to operate for over 96 years! When all was said and done the canal was still a cheap way to haul a slow load of coal from Cumberland to Georgetown and there seemed to be plenty of coal around to haul.

Chapter 6.

CHESAPEAKE AND OHIO CANAL: HEYDAY AND DEMISE

During the 22 years from 1858 to 1880 the Chesapeake and Ohio Canal enjoyed the height of its prosperity. The historian Walter Sanderlin calls it "The Golden Age of the Canal." At no other time during the history of the enterprise did the canal come so near to operating as a successful business venture. Canal tonnage rose from 167,000 tons in 1852, the second year of its full operation, to a tonnage of almost 1 million tons in 1875. For the first time the canal company began reducing some of the prior liens securing its burdensome debt. Net revenues totalled more than $200,000 each year from 1872 through 1875. The number of boats operating on the canal increased to almost 800.

So successful had the canal become that unloading and storage facilities in Georgetown became inadequate. Canal boats would pile up at the Georgetown level and increasing tonnage was difficult to handle. The backup of boats became a problem of major proportions for the boatmen impatiently waiting to unload at the coal wharves. James C. Clark, then president of the company, reported to the stockholders in December 1871:

As it is now, it is not infrequently the case that from sixty to eighty boats have to lie along the Canal bank singly so as to allow sufficient room in the

Canal boats jammed at Georgetown. (Courtesy of the National Park Service)

Canal for boats to pass in opposite directions. Often a string of unloaded boats from half a mile to a mile in length is seen lying above the Collector's Office in Georgetown, waiting their turn to get to the wharves to discharge their cargoes. (Sanderlin 1946:227–228)

Canallers and their families pitched camps along the banks of the river, making great stirrings by day and songs and laughter continuing far into the night.

The last slow mile of the journey through Georgetown to the Potomac River took three to four hours at best. There had to be a better and quicker way to transfer boats from the canal to the river. Thus, the Georgetown Outlet Incline was invented by the canal company's chief engineer, William R. Hutton. Hutton's ingenious invention was constructed by the Potomac Lock and Dock Company and the machinery at the Vulcan Iron Works in Baltimore. The incline was located at the edge of the towpath, one mile above the Aqueduct Bridge in Georgetown. It was the largest structure of its kind in the world and was well known in European engineering circles. Some years after the Paris Exposition, drawings of the Outlet Incline were

Rare photograph of the Outlet Incline. (Courtesy of the National Park Service)

included in a two-volume work on canals and notable achievements in canal engineering, *Rivers and Harbors,* published in Oxford in 1896. Copies of these volumes can be found in the library of the U.S. Naval Academy in Annapolis, Maryland.

The Outlet Incline was a cable-car affair. Canal boats carrying as much as 130 tons of coal destined to be off-loaded at points on the Georgetown wharves, nearby, inched their way into a large water-tight car called a caisson at the top of the incline. The total weight of the loaded canal boat and the water-filled caisson topped 400 tons. Excess water in the closed lock was then released and the huge mass slowly dropped 40 feet, at an $8\frac{1}{2}$ percent grade, to the river below. Energy to operate the Incline machinery was supplied by a steam engine and a winch. There were three sets of tracks, one in the center to carry the heavy caisson and its cargo and two additional sets on either side of the caisson to carry cars on wheels loaded with stone and used as counterweights. Steam towboats waited at the river level to move canal boats to their destinations after they were released from the caisson. Canal boats returning upstream were handled in reverse.

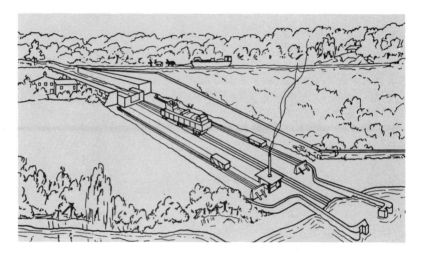

Outlet Incline 1876–1889, Chesapeake and Ohio Canal. (Illustration by Jan Thomas)

The entire operation, one-way, took 10 minutes. While there were accidents, the Outlet Incline worked and transported some 2,000 canal boats during its 13 years of operation from 1876 to 1889.

Between May 30 and June 1, 1889, a colossal flood swept down the Potomac. Its crest was higher than any previously recorded in the history of the valley. This flood is sometimes referred to as the Flood of the Johnstown Rains. The rains falling in the Potomac Basin were the same rains that fell over Johnstown, Pennsylvania. The deluge caused havoc in several watersheds throughout parts of Maryland, Virginia, the Ohio Valley, and Pennsylvania. Pennsylvania's Connemaugh Valley was particularly hard hit where the city of Johnstown received its crushing blow from the waters that poured from the breached dam high above the city.

Canal boats were lost and there was no doubt that the canal would go into receivership this time. The Chesapeake and Ohio Canal Company accepted bankruptcy, unable to raise funds to restore the canal. The Baltimore and Ohio Railroad Company emerged as the majority owner of both the 1878 and 1844 bonds, thereby giving it control of the preferred mortgages on the physical property and future revenues from all canal operations.

After the flood, the canal lay like a corpse, the whitest of white elephants. Rumors began to fly and there was much speculation as to the future of the canal's skeletal remains and its valuable right-of-way. Under the threat of a forced sale, the Baltimore and Ohio Railroad knuckled under and agreed to repair the canal, putting it in operating condition again to insure that the canal right-of-way would not fall into the hands of competitors standing in the wings, even if the canal had to be operated at a loss. Here began the annual ritual of proving to the court that the canal was being kept in ready operating condition, whether or not there was coal traffic, and that the canal was a viable concern, fully capable of meeting its obligations under a mountain of debt. Thus, the charter could be retained, competition held at bay, and prior rights to the water in the Potomac River required for navigation guaranteed.

Although the canal lay lifeless, it was a valuable asset. The federal government and the State of Maryland were the principal subscribers to the stock of the Chesapeake and Ohio Canal Company. Most of the money to build the canal had been advanced by Maryland and secured by mortgages. The canal charter was held by the courts to be a compact among Virginia, Maryland, and the federal government. Therefore, any breach of the charter could only benefit the states that granted it. The court held that all the powers granted to the now defunct Potomac Company, which the Chesapeake and Ohio Canal Company had assumed, in governing the control of the Potomac Valley and its waters, were expected to be in perpetuity and only revocable by the concurrent action of the three sovereign entities that had entered into the compact. Thus, when the C & O Canal was later purchased by the federal government in 1938, it was purchased as a viable concern, which included the right to withdraw from the Potomac River all the water required for navigation.

Repairs, as a result of the 1889 flood, reached a total cost of $435,000, an extraordinary sum for those days, especially as this was all borrowed money. Water was readmitted in August 1891. The Canal Towage Company was then organized to bring order to the canal and to gain control over freight charges. But the era of the independent boatman was almost over. Although there were some remaining independents left, they could not compete against the large

Henry Williams and Andy Jenkins operated a canal boat out of Hancock, Maryland. (Courtesy of the National Park Service)

There are few photographs of canallers and their families taken before the 1889 floods. In 1889 photography was still relatively in its infancy. Cameras were bulky, and the heavy wet collodion plates were too expensive for working-class canal families. Besides, canallers seldom considered their mules and boats to be fit subjects for photographing. Almost all the old pictures of canal life we see today were taken after 1889 and even then few former boat owners can be positively identified.

There are, however, many stories of canal life still alive to give us a close look at those difficult days. The few canallers left tell us that the canal families, of necessity, were close and administered to the sick among themselves. The men knew the names of the wives and children of their companion boatmen, the names of their mules, and the numbers assigned to each canal boat.

Canallers were hard-working family folk with a unique way of life that grew few roots. During the winter layovers, families were confined to their 12-foot-square boat cabins, often iced in. They tended to tie up either at the Cumberland basin or small basins along the way where relatives might live nearby. A few canal families had homes in small towns like Hancock or Sharpsburg, and some better-off independents had more than one boat, but this was the exception. Canal families led hard lives. Young children were expected to do the work of adults with no pay.

Two black canallers, Henry Williams and Andy Jenkins, operated a canal boat out of Hancock. They were employees of the Consolidated Coal Company and their boat belonged to the company. Henry Williams had nine children and there was plenty of help around when the boat was operating. Harnesses had to be cleaned and repaired, the mules had to be walked to Georgetown and back, or the second team of mules run down the plank to the towpath to be fed and harnessed for their turn at the towrope.

Canal life was simply accepted. It was hardly romantic or even desirable, so say the few canallers who are still with us today, recalling the sting of the ice on the towrope on early morning fall days and the swarms of green flies over the towpath in the oppressive heat of summer. In addition, there were the endless and tedious treks to Georgetown and the return, the drudgery of the daily grooming of the mules, and the paltry wages.

In the days of the independent canallers before 1889, boats were well cared for and a 93-foot canal boat could be slipped into a 100-foot lock, slick as a whistle, with no scraping or bilging. Locks were seldom more than 15 feet wide with only inches to spare between the boat and the insides of the locks. This allowed for quick passage through the lock with no time lost filling unnecessary water voids. The boatmen seldom hit the inside of a lock for fear of being fined by the company.

When going downstream, called "locking down," the canal boat would float into the filled lock chamber and the upstream gates would close. The canal boat would come to a stop in the chamber through the use of snubbing lines that were wound around snubbing posts planted along the tops of the locks. Snubbing lines could be cinched and acted as brakes. Butterfly gates were opened at the bottom of the downstream lock gate and water would rush out until the lock had barely enough water in it to float the boat out. The downstream lockgate would open and the boat would then proceed on its way. Boats coming upstream would reverse the procedure. All this took about ten minutes, each way.

Boats going downstream had the right-of-way. An approaching

boat, going upstream, would drop its towing line to the bottom of the canal. The boat going downstream would pass over the line and then proceed down-canal on the way to its destination.

Consolidation Coal Company that owned most of the Georges Creek coal fields.

Consolidation Coal Company was owned, in turn, by the Baltimore and Ohio Railroad. The Canal Towage Company offered a convenience, but this company, too, was a part of the mighty conglomerate that now provided boats and mules to experienced boatmen. The Canal Towage Company controlled and regulated schedules, and imposed unpopular standards of operation on both their own boat captains and the few independents who were left. Each boat was numbered and its trips down the canal and back were tightly scheduled. The individualistic flair that marked the close-knit independent canal families before the 1889 floods disappeared in time. In their places were former boatmen who had lost everything in the flood, and the host of near-destitute but willing canal families who knew no other life.

Finally the State of Maryland, owning most of the property, decided to sell its vast interest in the C & O Canal for whatever it could get. The Western Maryland Railway Company paid $115,000 for the $2 million loan rights and $5 million in canal stock. The deal was consummated in 1905, but within two years the Western Maryland Railroad went into receivership and the old arch rival Baltimore and Ohio Railroad once again gained ownership and the relationship between the receivers and the B & O continued as it had been before.

On March 29, 1924, the first major flood in 35 years swept down the valley. Melting snows and heavy rains caused major overflowing of the canal's banks. Valley newspapers correctly blamed the flood on heavy timber cutting, which had denuded much of the Allegheny watershed in western West Virginia and Maryland. A second flood followed and by this time it was obvious that the demise of the canal was at hand. The floods provided the opportunity for the Baltimore and Ohio Railroad to discontinue operating the canal, and the receivers made no effort to restore the canal beyond its Georgetown

Mule teams, groomed and ready for a day's work. (Courtesy of the National Park Service)

Cushwa's wharf at Williamsport on the C & O Canal. (Courtesy of the National Park Service)

level. The receivers then authorized just enough work to put the canal back into operating condition, making sure the Georgetown millers had the required amount of water needed to generate power. Although the canal was a wreck, it was still, technically, a viable concern, and the court continued to so rule. Georges Creek coal had been depleted in amounts significant enough for any realistic return to the coal trade as the canal had experienced it at one time. The canal quickly fell into decay. The flood of 1936 finished off what was left, and the ditch remained a hulk for two years until the federal government struck a deal to acquire it for $2 million. This was the approximate amount needed by the B & O Railroad to cover payments on a Reconstruction Finance Corporation loan for which the canal had been pledged as security.

The Chesapeake and Ohio Canal Company earned little for its investors during its 96 years of operation. In this sense the canal was a colossal failure, but not for the users of the canal. During its heyday in its peak year, 1871, the canal transported a record 968,827 tons of cargo and over 800 boats operated on the waterway. Between 1858 and 1880, the canal reached the peak of its prosperity. The good days saw numerous general merchandise and feed stores at many of the locks. Warehouses and additional unloading facilities were constructed. In 1879, one of the first private industrial telephone systems was built along the entire length of the canal.

The turmoil of the river and canal was finally over. Years of hard work and tenuous financial stress, spanning the presidential terms of George Washington to Franklin D. Roosevelt, came to an end. A possible route to the Ohio River became a National Historical Park in less than four generations, with each generation, including today's, beset by financial shortages, destructive floods, and deteriorating resources.

Chapter 7.

LIFE ALONG THE RIVER

It is pleasant to embark upon a voyage if only for the day. Your boat becomes a moving studio and you can carry so many things with you. It is almost as if you put out oars at your windows to move your house along . . . Henry David Thoreau, 1831

CHARLES MILL

The art of milling in this country is, and was, not only a business, but a culture closely allied to the times and ways of the Old World. Country water mills were essential additions to rural agricultural communities and the ever-increasing number of mills in this country reached a peak of 100,000 by the mid-nineteenth century. Here is a look at one of the few old mills remaining with its original mill seat intact, the oldest in Washington County, Maryland, and an uninterrupted family milling lineage dating to 1814.

Charles Mill and its surrounding community are located on the berm side of the C & O Canal, about a half-mile below the settlement of Four Locks, and 3 miles south of Clear Spring, Maryland, at a point where Camp Springs Run empties into the Potomac River. (The Charles Mill should not be confused with another mill 20 miles downriver, which is also sometimes referred to as Charles Mill, title having passed through several owners, including the Charles family.)

Back in the early 1950s, when I first saw the mill, it looked intact. I recall a landing and a basin on the canal side of the structure. Understandably, time and floods have taken their toll, but original foundation stones are still in place marking the precise outlines of the

Charles Mill. (Courtesy of the National Park Service)

original mill building. The miller's house is presently occupied by Janet Charles. Bernhard and Janet Charles's five children were raised on the mill property, making them the seventh generation of the Charles family to live at the mill. Mrs. Charles graciously recounted the stories of the great milling days at Camp Springs Run, and discussed the many contributions to the surrounding community that the various Charles families made over a considerable amount of time, from 1814 to the present.

Milling at the Charles Mill site is said to date back to the days of General Braddock, and its products would have certainly been transported by longboats down the Potomac River to Georgetown during the busy days of George Washington's Patowmack Company. The country mill was at the center of local rural economies, providing a tangible means of turning grain harvests into cash or trade goods. Farmers brought their products to the mill to be ground, and in payment, the mill owner, by custom, exacted a share of the products ranging from about one-tenth to one-fourth, depending on the kind of product processed, plus any services rendered. The various Charles families, in addition to operating a flourishing standing grist mill, ground plaster that also served as ballast on passing canal boats. There was also a sawmill operation, probably on land where the C & O Canal was built; and a cooper shop where barrels were made to store and ship flour. Barrels were sold for 33½ cents each. As was customary, most millers did a bit of farming, usually raising wheat and livestock. Mill locations along the canal and the river were ideal, with eager markets for flour and other products downriver in Georgetown.

The Charles Mill was supplied with power from a great over-shot water wheel. Water from nearby Big Spring flowed through a flat trough, called a millrace. The water overshot the top of the water wheel, then fell into wide troughs attached to the perimeter of the wheel. The sheer weight of the water-filled troughs slowly turned the powerful wheel. When the water in the troughs reached the bottom of the wheel, it poured out into a stream flowing under the wheel, then into the river. A huge wooden shaft, hand-hewn from the trunk of a tree, was the foundation upon which the wooden wheels were built. The arms were mortised into the shaft, then the outside circle of the wheel buckets and rims were fitted upon it.

One of the important steps in assuring the durability of wooden water wheels was called "ironing the wheel." Ironing involved fastening metal journal pieces, called gudgeons, onto the ends of a wooden shaft. The stirrup portion of the gudgeon, resting on the opposite stone foundations, supported each end of the hub or shaft.

The ironed shaft, passing through the gudgeon in the foundation wall, connected with the line-shaft or pulley wheel on the inside of the mill. In Charles Mill today, the inside wheel is fairly intact. Line shaft-driven belts were capable of distributing power to various stories and locations of a mill. The great leather belts were installed by hand lacing, a tedious and highly skilled task that, fortunately, did not require frequent repetition. The shaft of Charles Mill is remembered as having a wooden cogwheel that meshed with other wooden cogs with such loud knocking sounds that they could be heard throughout the mill valley.

Wheat was ground into flour. Barley, corn, and rye were ground for horses and cows. Farmers drove their wagons into a passageway under the mill. The grain was lifted from the wagons into the mill. Both the mill owner and the farmers kept detailed accounts of the amount of flour received, and the wheat they had left with the miller. Each time the farmer received this flour or other product, it was noted in the books. Grain to be ground for feed was paid for by the bushel, but it was tolled, one-tenth of a bushel to be kept by the miller to pay for grinding. Grinding the grain for cattle was done on the "buhrs" or millstones, made of flint and very heavy. They were as large as 5 feet in diameter. The top stone rested and turned on the bottom stone. Grain entered through an opening in the center of the upper stone, and the turning stone slung it to the outer edge where it fell into a spout and then into a sack. The upper stone could be raised or lowered to obtain a proper texture. If corn was ground for cornmeal the process was the same, except that the spout scarring the ground meal led to a sifter in the floor below the millstones. The sifter was attached to an eccentric shaft, giving the contraption a swift back and forth motion, separating the hull from the meal. To obtain buckwheat flour, the process was the same as that for cornmeal, except that the black, sharp-edged grain was fed into the stone buhr instead of corn and a finer sieve was slipped into the sifter. Buckwheat flour was finer in texture than cornmeal, and had a rich dark color all its own.

The cumbersome millstones had to be "dressed" or sharpened periodically. The stone was lifted high so that when it was turned, the grinding surface was on top. Both grinding surfaces had to be made rough enough to grind grain. Tempered sharp hammers that cut into the flint millstones produced the new grooves in the grinding surfaces. This process could take as long as two days.

Steel rollers were also used to make flour from wheat instead of millstones. Wheat was fed between two rollers, one running faster than the other. The "sifting" was done by "bolting clothes" of very fine mesh made of silk, forming the outside of a large cylinder that turned around. The fine flour sifted through, and the coarse material went back to the rollers to be ground again.

There were three main products left when the roller mill had finished with the wheat: the flour, which was finely textured and very white, the bran from the outside hull of the wheat, and last, the middlings (wheat germ). Whole wheat flour was little known in those days. People used the flour, cows ate the bran, and pigs ate the middlings.

No flour bleaching was done in the mill, but the miller had to test for whiteness, using a "flour slick," a piece of flat, shiny metal, looking much like a flat metal shoehorn, which the miller carried in his pocket. By passing the flour slick over the flour held in his hand, the miller could see specks. If too many specks showed up in his flour slick test, the mill was stopped and repairs were then made to any holes in the silk bolting clothes.

The brand of flour shipped from Charles Mill was Daisy Mills Flour, first placed in barrels but later placed in flour bags with "Daisy Mills" imprinted on the front.

In time there were three mills on the original Charles tract: Bell's Mill, Kuhn's Mill, and the "lower" mill, which was continuously owned and operated by the Charles family. When the C & O Canal ceased operations in 1924, the most economical method of transporting the flour to market was lost, ending seven generations of mill activities.

TRIP OF THE NEW *RUDDER GRANGE* ON THE CHESAPEAKE AND OHIO CANAL

What was a canal boat excursion really like just before the turn of the century? Here are real-life scenes from the diary of William Wallace Frantz of a pleasure jaunt up-canal and back, along with the innocent thoughts of its enthusiastic passengers, young and old.

On the morning of August 23, 1894, William Wallace Frantz and friends boarded a canal boat, the *Rudder Grange,* at McCoy's Ferry, not far from the community of Clear Spring, Maryland. With their oil stove, bedding, and plenty of good food aboard, they were pulled 48 miles upstream by alternating teams of mules until they reached the upper end of the Paw Paw Tunnel, 29 towpath-miles below Cumberland, Maryland. The party then turned around and returned to

Boat in lock. (Helmer Collection)

McCoy's Ferry. William Wallace Frantz (1861–1941) tells a charming tale, never before published. Here is life as it really was along the river and canal during those uncomplicated days of the late nineteenth century.

Thursday morning, August 23, 1894, we arose early and drove to McCoy's Ferry, four miles Southwest of Laurel Hill [the Frantz home was built 1 mile north of Clear Spring]. The ferry is so named because the McCoy's owned and operated a ferry-boat between the Maryland and West Virginia sides of the Potomac river at this point. We had three wagon loads of goods: food and clothing and bedding, live freight, etc.

All who expected to take the trip were on hand by nine O'clock. A short time was spent in stowing away the goods, melons, etc., and in decorating the boat and putting up the awnings.

At ten A.M., with many cheers and "good byes," we cast loose our moorings and started westward over the historic old water-way.

Our boat was named for the occasion, after Frank R. Stockton's interesting novel, *The Rudder Grange*.

The boat was propelled by four mules in relays of two at a time. While two are pulling the boat by a tow line 60 or 80 feet long, two are in the forward cabin resting and eating. They exchange teams every 15 or 20 miles. They bring the two out of the cabin, and the two that have been on the tow path are run in on a narrow gang-plank and down a board, like steps into the cabin. When the mules go down one of the men catches hold of their tails to steady them and keep them from breaking their necks.

Three men composed the crew: the captain, first mate or steersman, and Slicky, the tow-boy.

The boat was gaily decorated with large and small flags, and bunting in the national colors, and the flag staff was topped by a large streamer on which was the name of the boat.

Three large canvasses, covering half the deck, sheltered us from the sun's rays and protected us from the dew and cool night breezes. We also had the use of two cabins. One, containing two rooms, was general utility cabin; the other was used for store-room and kitchen. We had an oil stove with us and also had the use of a cooking stove on the boat, upon which breakfast was cooked every morning. We had hot coffee every meal.

Our first stop was made at old Fort Frederick, three miles from our starting point. Time was given for the party to inspect this old relic of the "French and Indian" war. It is on a gentle slope, three hundred yards from the canal, overlooking the Baltimore and Ohio R.R., the Potomac river, and Big Pool (a small lake, fed by the canal, one and one-half miles long and three-fourths mile wide, the resort of duck hunters and fishermen from far and near).

The Fort was built by Governor Sharpe just after Braddock's defeat near Fort Duquesne in 1856, to protect the settlers from marauding Indians who had become very bold and driven many settlers to fly even as far as Baltimore.

The Fort is built in the form of a square with protruding block corners and contains about three acres. The walls are four and one-half feet thick at base and three feet at top and fifteen feet high. They are built of rough stone collected in the immediate vicinity and cement sent from England to St. Mary's town in sailing vessels, and from there it was taken up the river in flat bottomed boats, that required a great amount of manual labor to pole and pull against the current of the river.

Fort Frederick is memorable [as] the place in which some British soldiers, captured at the surrender of Cornwallis at Yorktown, were imprisoned, and because it was built under the direction of Washington, upon a spot then on the "Western Frontier." A company of Union soldiers were stationed there, with several heavy guns, to protect the B & O R.R., during the late war.

It is now owned by a . . . family named Williams who used it for a grape vineyard for many years. They now have it in grass with many young shade trees growing nicely. It is a favorite place for picnics, dances, etc.

The walls are in a fair state of preservation except where they built a barn on one wall.

We sailed through Big Pool, past Cherry Run, Licking Creek (which some of the party called Kissing Creek), Old Mill Stone Point (so-called from the indians killing a man here while he was at work dressing a mill burr), through Little Pool, ate our dinner on the deck of the boat, and reached Hancock at 2:30 P.M.

We stopped at this beautiful little town, named for John Hancock, of Revolutionary fame, about forty minutes, and were joined by several young ladies, who accompanied us on the remainder of the trip.

We passed the *Oriole*, Hancock's little pleasure boat, a short distance up and were followed by it as far as the cement mills, where it stopped, to return to Hancock that night.

Heretofore, the trip has been through low farming lands with the mountains blue in the distance, but now the scenery changes. We are in the mountains. Just across the river is the famous Lover's Leap while here on our right are perpendicular walls of rock, rising hundreds of feet, and coming so close that we can often reach out and touch them. We can look back toward the heart of the mountains in caverns, artificial and natural, some of which run back for two miles. In one cave can be seen a family of owls, who, when aroused, blink their moon eyes at passing boats.

We reached Dam No. 6, one of the feeders of the canal, with Little Capon Village just across the river on the B. & O. R.R., just after dark, and anchored a few miles west, soon after passing Possum Hollow: a cold North wind was blowing down the Hollow and made everyone look for wraps and overcoats; but as soon as we came under the shelter of the mountains again, we were very comfortable.

The sides and ends of the canvasses were closed and plenty of mattresses, blankets, and comforts [sic] were spread on the deck for sleeping purposes. The girls changed their dresses in the cabin for wrappers, (principally red), and all were in bed by 10.30. The girls could not be kept from talking, so it was next to impossible to sleep. Nearly all managed to obtain four or five hours sleep.

Some of the party arose at two oclock A.M. and the boat starting, about four oclock, roused all.

It was certainly strange to hear the calls of the boatmen and creaking of rudders through the fog, with now and then a solitary horn blowing "lock-ready," while just across the river were the flashing lights and loud rumblings of the trains, passing every five or ten minutes, on the B. & O. R.R.

We passed a small village, Little Orleans, just after daylight and soon after entered Alleghany county. Sideling Hill Creek is the dividing line.

Some of the party left the boat at a lock, to take a walk on the tow-path, before breakfast. To get back on the boat they had to walk up a steep, narrow plank moved along by the boat at one end while the other rested on the tow-path. As each girl was assisted up, the lower end of the plank was raised and carried forward to catch up with the boat again. We were not so careful with the boys and the first one who attempted it was dipped into the cool water, by the upper end of the plank leaving the boat very suddenly. This is known among boatmen as running the plank. The unlucky gentleman scrambled out and on to the boat, where he was supplied with a full outfit of dry clothes, after which he felt none the worse for his involuntary plunge.

We purchased a quart of fresh milk, from a woman, at a house about a hundred feet above our heads, on a very steep hill, and every-one enjoyed a breakfast of: Eggs, hard and soft-boiled and raw; potatoes with jackets on, because of the cool morning; beef, chicken, ham, rolls, buscuits [sic], coffee, cantaloupes, etc, etc, etc, etc, etc.

In shaking out the table cloths, one of the young ladies, forgetting she was not on terra firma, let one table cloth and a silver spoon fall overboard when they sank immediately, never to be heard of more. One of the party went swimming to try to find the cloth, but without success.

We reached Paw Paw tunnel, the objective point of the excursion, at noon. Forty-eight miles from McCoy's Ferry.

There are 16 locks from McCoy's Ferry to the tunnel, with an average fall of nine feet to the lock. Allowing two and one half feet to the mile for flow of water, we raise two hundred and thirty-two feet. Quite a raise for a water-way.

While waiting for another boat to come out of the tunnel, some of the party obtained a supply of the coldest water I have ever tasted. It is from a beautiful spring on the side of the mountain. The entrance to the tunnel is between great walls of solid slate rock, almost perpendicular for nearly a hundred feet. The eastern entrance is almost a quarter of a mile between these cliffs, which are so close that two boats cannot pass. The tunnel itself is three thousand four hundred feet long, twenty-five feet wide and twenty-five feet high, with a narrow wooden tow-path along one side and a depth of eight feet of water. The walls are of brick and cement, forty-five inches in thickness. The tunnel is perfectly straight and was one of the greatest engineering feats of the day, being excavated from three points; each end a shaft sunk from the top of the mountain to the middle of the tunnel.

Small stalactites hang from the ceiling, although the walls are perfectly dry at this time.

As soon as we reached wide water on the western side of the mountain, we turned round and began our homeward journey. We sang songs, shouted, played the boat horn and gave our yells of:

> "Hobble gobble, razzle dazzle,
> Sis boom bah;
> Clearspring, Clearspring,
> 'Rah, 'tah, 'rah"
> and

"Hager, Hager, Hager,
Sis boom bang;
'Rah, 'Rah, 'Rah,
Clearspring gang"

to awake the echoes and were silent awhile listening to the ripple of the water.

We were accompanied through the tunnel by an ex-soldier, who said he had had the fortune, or misfortune, of being captured and put in Rebel prisons three times. He met and spoke to Sheridan on his famous ride to the battle of Cedar Creek. He was very talkative, and a great believer in the up and down signs of the moon. He advised all to get married in the up of the moon to live happily.

We replenished our water supply at the spring and ate our fourth meal on the boat. The menu consisted of: Roasting ears, sliced tomatoes, sour catophel [cataphyll?], meats, melons, etc, etc, etc, etc

We reviewed the beautiful scenery of the morning and anchored at Little Orleans for the night, when some of the party sought the river to take a bath by the light of a lantern.

They enjoyed themselves, even if it was dark.

Everybody seemed more sleepy than the night before and prepared for bed earlier.

All slept well and we did not start until six oclock, because we wanted to see the scenery, we had passed in the night, going up. The survey of the proposed Baltimore and Cumberland railroad follows the course of the canal here, for several miles, along almost perpendicular bluffs from fifty to one hundred and fifty feet high.

One contractor proposed to blow this immense quantity of rock, over the canal and into the river without obstructing the canal. He proposed to use dynamite, in a long serries [sic] of holes, to be set off all at once by means of an electric battery. Other contractors said it was impossible.

We passed, this morning, a handsome cottage and a fine clubhouse on the wooded hills that slope up from the canal on the North [the Woodmont Club]. They are owned by wealthy Washington people, who spend a part of every summer there.

We passed Dam No. 6 at nine oclock, where we obtained fresh water from a spring in the bed of the river. A glass was inverted, dipped to the bottom, turned "right side up with care," and brought up filled with sparkling spring-water.

When we boarded the boat, some of the party borrowed costumes and gave us quite an exhibition of talent. They gave us "Sweet Marea," and other popular songs of the day, interspersed with recitations and cornet solos, by the leader, Harry Van Dyke.

They received a great deal of well-merited applause and many encores.

. . . We arrived at the Cement Mills at eleven oclock. Here is quite an extensive industry.

The cement rock is dug from mines extending far back under "Little Round Top" mountain [three canal-miles above Hancock]. It is put in kilns with limestone and burned with coal and wood, after which it is ground and barreled, when it is shipped all over the country via the B. & O. R.R. and the C. & O. Canal. They have a warehouse across the river on the railroad, to which the cement is carried on inclined cables of great strength.

"Round Top" cement was used on Congressional Library, War, State and Navy buildings and other public works in Washington.

Just across the river on the West Virginia shore are the "Sand Banks," where white sandstone is mined and quarried and shipped to Pittsburg and other points, for the manufacture of glass.

"Lovers Leap" is just below this place on the bank of the Potomac and above the B.& O. R.R.

It is said that when this country was first settled a young white man met and fell in love with a beautiful Indian princess. The feeling was reciprocated and they were perfectly happy, until a shadow, in the shape of the old chief, fell athwart their path.

Prompted by a jealous young Indian, who was in love with the girl, he forbade their meeting. They soon surmounted this barrier and for a long time, met clandestinely at Lover's Leap, where they could look out over the beautiful Potomac Valley and gaze into each other's souls through the eyes. They went to this Lover's paradise every evening until the girl's absence was noticed and the young Indian, following her one evening, saw their meeting and informed the old chief, who, the next evening, collected a few braves and surrounded the couple out on the point of the rocks. There was no way to escape, so the lovers resolved to jump over the rocks and die together, rather than to be separated. They clasped their arms around each other, and threw themselves over the cliff and were crushed to death on the rocks below. Thus runs the "Legend of the Potomac."

Here we took leave of the most rugged and magnificent scenery of the trip, to be exchanged for the varied landscapes and beautiful views of an agricultural country. The greater part of the trip was with great precipices of rock on the Northern bank of the canal, from whose tops great rocks were hurled down at passing boats below, during times of strikes on the canal, but whose sides, in these more peaceful times, were covered with morning glories, wild clematis, air plant, gentian, and many other varieties of beautiful wild flowers in bloom, interspersed here and there with a few stunted cedar and pine trees.

All this was now changed. Large corn fields, peach orchards, low farmhouses, etc comprised the principal features of the scenery, with the ever changing view of the river and its many tributaries.

We reached Hancock at twelve oclock, where the ladies, who had joined us on our upward way, took leave of our party. Here we were joined by Mrs. Bricker and Helen, wife and daughter of one of our party from Chambersburg.

We passed Little Pool and Old Millstone Point and reached the Big Pool, just below Cherry Run, in time to allow our chaperon and her son to get aboard the five Oclock train for their home in Hagerstown.

After a swift sail down the Pool, a stop was made at the Fort long enough for some of the party who were provided with suits, to take a dip in the waters of the old canal. A gold hatpin that had been accidentally dropped overboard was restored uninjured to the owner, by one of the bathers.

We reached the home landing all too soon, where we cheered and gave our yells in our best style. We were not long in disembarking, however, and were driven home with our luggage in the waiting wagons and carriages, arriving at home [Clear Spring] about eight by the clock . . .

[Passengers:] Misses Etta H. Adams, Mollie Booze and Florence and May Rothrock, of Baltimore; Katie Emmart of Washington; Nettie Duffield and Carrie Ditto, Welsh Run, Pa.; Sallie Perry and Maggie Hill, Elizabeth City, N.C.; Ida, Alice, and Loutie Beard, Maria Draper, Lillian Reed, Mollie, Emma and Julia Frantz, Estella and Marea Powers, Clearspring, Md.; and Mrs. Wise, chaperon of Hagerstown, Md.

Messrs. W. H. Bricker and Harry Sierer, Chambersburg, Pa.; Ned Wise, Hagerstown; John Meany, Washington; C.B. Ditto and B. F. Royer, Welsh Run, Pa.; B. J. Boswell and Will, Ed, Gilmore and Harry Frantz of Clearspring.

At Hancock we were joined by Nellie and Lillian Perkins, Ethel Swingle and May Creager of that place, and Mr. F. B. Thomas of Johnstown, Pa.

On our return trip Mrs. Bricker and Helen joined us at Hancock.

MAGNOLIA

For years I had been floating past remnants of what must have been a unique community. I was always curious, watching it recover from floods with their unceasing devastation . . . then I learned that this was, long ago, a community especially developed for the families who worked for the railroads, complete with a mission of its own, quite unlike any story I had ever heard. I couldn't resist the urge to find out more.

"If there were more people living in Magnolia like there used to be, I'd be back there in a minute," says Alice Myers who presently

Waiting for the train, B & O Station, Magnolia, May 30, 1904. (Courtesy of the National Park Service)

makes her home in Paw Paw, West Virginia. "Magnolia was bigger than Paw Paw at one time when they put the works through for the High Line. I guess there were over 2,000 people living there then. Some people stayed and some left, on account of the work stopping." Alice Myers expresses the same affection for Magnolia that other folks do. There is always a twinkle in her eye when she recounts the good days, long ago, when she was growing up in this unique and close-knit community.

Magnolia is a quiet place located along the West Virginia bank of the Potomac River, 7 miles downriver from Paw Paw. In 1838, Baltimore and Ohio Railroad construction had reached Magnolia, some 38 river-miles below Cumberland, Maryland. A water station, signal tower, and depot were built here. Magnolia's first post office was established at Water Station No. 12 from 1863 to 1864. James Riley was postmaster. Water Station No. 12 serviced the steam engines by providing water drawn from the river for the engine's water tenders. Water Station No. 12 became a "helper station," providing standby engines to assist through-trains in climbing the steep Doe Gully grade, located several miles below Magnolia. In 1867, the post office was renamed Magnolia Vale. Later, in 1871, it reopened as Magnolia. In the late 1800s a steam mill was operating, and in 1887, Isaac Wilson built a large granary here. In 1903, the Western Maryland Railroad began construction in this area.

In 1910, Magnolia boomed when the B & O Railroad began the construction of the "Magnolia Cut-off," also called the "High Line." Three construction companies, including the American Bridge Company, were located in Magnolia. Four great tunnels were built: Randolph, Stuart, and Graham in Maryland, and Carothers in West Virginia. Two bridges spanning the Potomac River were also constructed in the vicinity of Magnolia. Three section crews worked out of Magnolia just to maintain the tracks.

The first dispatcher's office for the Cumberland division of the B & O was located in Magnolia. Two others followed, one down the tracks at Orleans Crossroads (across from Little Orleans, Maryland); and another up the tracks at Okonoko, West Virginia. All three had interlocking towers, and received direction from the chief dispatcher in Cumberland. Dispatchers in the towers set switches manually, as instructed over wirephones, moving great levers attached to connecting rods, which produced track cut-offs, or bypasses, within the Magnolia complex, designed for the trains to avoid or pass through certain tunnels or travel over selected bridges to seek the most advantageous distances to destinations. In later years the system was automated, and now operates from Cumberland, 38 miles up the tracks from Magnolia.

At the peak of construction, times were good in Magnolia. Railroad workers went to work on self-propelled railroad handcarts. Alice Myers speaks of two churches, a two-room schoolhouse, a movie hall, grocery stores, general merchandise stores, a barber shop, a doctor's office, a drug store, and a butcher shop. Folks living in Magnolia bought beautiful plants from a man across the river in Maryland. All you had to do was call out, she said, and he would come over in his boat to make a sale.

During construction of the Graham Tunnel, a swinging bridge was strung across the river, used by workers on their way to work in the morning, and by those with a keen thirst in the evening. The bridge led to a saloon on the Maryland side, and when you saw the man of the house making his way across the bridge in the evening, there was no mistaking his intentions.

Alice Myers was born in Magnolia, and lived there almost all of her life. During the peak of prosperity, Maggie Norton Johnson operated a boardinghouse, and it is thought that Magnolia was named for Maggie and her sister, Nora Norton. The cut-off was completed in 1914. Many families moved out, their houses torn down, and loaded on railroad cars and moved to the next major construction site. In that same year a devastating fire destroyed eleven buildings. By 1919, Magnolia was listed as having a population of only fifty persons and two businesses. In 1927, the railroad station was torn down. Other families were forced to relocate after the 1936 flood. Alice and her husband built their house high and safe, and escaped the worst of the floodwaters. Mr. Myers found himself stranded on a helper train several miles away as the floodwaters rose. He was unable to get to Magnolia for several days after the flood.

The road to Magnolia winds its way over several spurs on Sideling Hill, to reach a height of about 1,215 feet, where there are magnificent vistas of the Paw Paw Valley with the Potomac forming its loops below. A nearby lookout tower rises 2,029 feet above sea level, affording a most dramatic view of the almost uninhabited Paw Paw Valley. Paw Paw Bends is a recent name for the serpentine bends that twist 31 miles from Paw Paw to Fifteenmile Creek (Little Orleans). After World War II, fishermen and canoeists referred to the bends as the "goosenecks." Paw Paw Bends did not come into use until the end of the 1940s with the first waves of canoes to come down the river.

Describing a tract of land in the Bends, George Washington wrote "This tract lies on the Potomac River about 12 miles above the town of Bath [Berkeley Springs], and is in the shape of a horseshoe, the river running almost around it—two hundred acres of rich low grounds with a great abundance of walnut trees." Thus, we have yet a third name for the Bends from George Washington, "The Horseshoe Bends."

Magnolia was one of those railroad and orchard communities served by the railroad during the early days when the railroads were being built. There were several such communities lying along the railroad right-of-way. Trains or flatcars picked up railroad workers in the morning, took them to the nearest track laying, and then back home again at night. It was an early version of a commuter shuttle.

After the November 1985 flood, there wasn't much left of the waterfront at Magnolia except the Moon Glow Skating Rink bus. It was hauled down from Cumberland years ago. The Moon Glow bus picked up young roller skaters and transported them to the rink in Cumberland, then home again after the rink closed. It still wears its red, white, and blue colors, surviving floods and freshets.

The Paw Paw Tunnel cuts through the base spurs of Sorrel Ridge on the Maryland side of the river, eliminating 7 miles of towpath construction. Magnolia is on the West Virginia side of the river, in an area where no towpath exists on either side of the river. Alice and her father used to visit the canal now and then, and she recalls hearing the canal boat captains shouting "Heyyy lock!" from a distance: the clarion call to the lock tender to wake up and prepare the lock for a canal boat. She recalls hearing members of the crew playing their mouth harps and guitars. Her father always felt sad for the rootless canallers, and it is likely that the canallers felt sad for the folks in Magnolia who had lost their freedom and were tied to one place. But, then, Magnolia was a pretty good place to be tied to.

THUNDER IN THE MOUNTAINS, PLUNDER UNDERNEATH

A number of years ago the land in the vicinity of the Fairfax Stone had been systematically ravaged by strip mining. Now, in 1992, the entire area has been reclaimed and it looks handsome.

Highway U.S. 219 takes you 3.5 miles north from Thomas, West Virginia, to a brown metal sign on the east side of the road, directing you to the Fairfax Stone and the nearby community of Kempton, Maryland. The roads are hard gravel. A new $3/4$-mile road swings you around the "first fountain" in an arc ending in Kempton. The stone, Marker No. 1, marks the precise point at which the "first fountain" flows east across the meridian line, running northward from the Fair-

Landslides on the cliffs above the downstream end of the Paw Paw Tunnel occur periodically. In 1978 some 120,000 cubic yards of shale was removed at the lower end of the tunnel. (Courtesy of the National Park Service)

fax Stone. This marks the southwestern corner of the State of Maryland.

Only a handful of houses remain in Kempton and its most glorious days are over, yet because of the Fairfax Stone, the community receives a lot of visitors, perhaps in part from Gilbert Gude's book, *Where the Potomac Begins*, a popular and authoritative account of the history of these highlands. Visitors have always made pilgrimages to Kempton and the Fairfax Stone. For years, railroad trains carried visitors to the stone, which was considered a unique and worthwhile attraction.

My wife, Sarah, grew up in Parsons, West Virginia, just down Backbone Mountain to the west. Here are the headwaters of the Cheat River, which so interested George Washington on his 1784 journey to the Ohio Country. Parsons is the county seat of Tucker County and, for me, it is also the place from which I do my serious canoeing. Sarah's family home is my boat put-in and ending-point for extended canoe trips through the maze of rivers and streams that wind their courses through the surrounding mountains. There are six rivers that flow into Parsons: the Dry Fork, Laurel Fork, Glady Fork, Shavers Fork, the Blackwater River, and the Black Fork River. Leaving town in a hurry and heading north is the Cheat River, which is made up of the six rivers merging at Parsons. The Cheat, now infused with six water sources, rushes north toward the Monongahela River, and eventually finds its way to the Ohio, and then to the Mississippi. Most rivers flowing east from the Allegheny Front wind up in the Atlantic Ocean, while the rivers flowing north and west wind up in the Gulf of Mexico.

Sarah had two uncles who worked during the lumber boom of the 1900s. "Uncle June" was a sawyer and "Uncle Ed" was a saw filer. June and his cutting crew would saw the trees by day, and Ed spent all night sharpening the saws to be used by the crews the next day. Filers had to be good, and skilled ones were hard to come by. Filers were expected to have their own tools, and their files were locked up when not in use. Without sharp saws, productive tree cutting was virtually impossible. Cutting crews worked 10 hours a day for $1.50 a day. Saw filers earned slightly more but were expected to lay out twelve or more sharpened saws for each day's work. June and Ed finally got jobs on the Baltimore and Ohio Railroad, June at Rowlesburg and Uncle Ed in the yards at Grafton. Uncle Ed became a boilermaker and was required to crawl into the massive Mallet engines, when they were still insufferably warm, to repair leaks. Even when they cooled down the engine boilers could stay at 120 degrees Fahrenheit or more inside. I once asked Uncle Ed how long it took him to repair a routine boiler leak when it was still hot. "Not long, son," he replied, "not long."

In the Cheat Valley, logs were shunted down ice slides in the winter, then down the rivers to the sawmills. In later years, Shay steam engines criss-crossed the steep mountains, increasing production dramatically. Trees were felled by the cutting crews while "knot bumpers" cut off any remaining limbs. The logs were then skidded to railroad loading points secured by heavy chains and pulled by horse teams. All trees were clear-cut: fine northern red and white pines, maples, spruce, fir, and birch, to the walnuts, elms, and aspens of the central states that somehow had migrated to this corner of the Appalachians.

Early photographs of enormous tree stumps left in the wake of massive logging operations may depict as many as six crew members standing abreast a felled spruce or yellow poplar, 16 feet or more in diameter. Today, most foresters can take you to forest enclaves where original virgin timber still stands. Usually these areas are remote and it is obvious that the trees could not be successfully cut and pulled out of their inaccessible "holes." These primary stand trees are wondrous to see, and there are not many left in Maryland and West Virginia.

Mining in these mountains was always a highly desirable job, even before the days of the unions. There has always been a sense of security attached to mining that appeals especially to family men. With the pressures exerted by the unions, pay increased and safety requirements were enforced, making the dangerous days underground fewer. Many of today's young miners are college-trained, and finding a job in the mines is not as easy as it once was. A deep mine, the 750-foot deep Metikki Mine near Table Rock, some 19 miles northeast of Kempton, has opened, and it provides excellent paying jobs for those lucky enough to get on the rolls.

I have always had a keen interest in how mines are operated and have spent many hours talking to retired miners who worked mines up and down the slopes outside of Parsons. A typical mine was the little mine in the community of Benbush, at the base of the western slope of Backbone Mountain, not too far from the Fairfax Stone, up the road from Parsons. Old timers are always ready to talk about their days in the mines and their recall is astounding. The Benbush Mine, once owned by the Davis Coal and Coke Company, has been closed for years. The company operated many mines peppered throughout the Beaver Creek area.

Recently, I was fortunate enough to talk to a former supervisor who worked for Davis Coal and Coke and who remembers the Benbush Mine well. It was only 200 feet deep and produced coal from

Abandoned mine. (Courtesy of the Interstate Commission on the Potomac River Basin)

the Upper Freeport seam from which excellent "smithing" coal was extracted. When burned, this coal produced less than 2 percent ash and virtually no sulphur. Upper Freeport coal is common throughout the Backbone and highly desirable. It is unlikely, however, that any marketable amounts of Freeport are left in the Benbush Mine or others nearby.

Miners used hand-cranked drills with short and long bits to reach the coal. Each miner carried a "powder sack" in which were carried "squibs" (caps for detonation) and a small supply of carbide for a miner's light, which was worn on the head. Although the use of dynamite and black powder was discontinued about 1922, many permissible substitutes became available. Monobel was a substitute powder used and was considered about 32 percent as effective as dynamite. Black powder or dynamite caused over-blasting, which caused serious damage to the mines and structures. Backfiring from an explosion would fill the mine with clouds of black dust and noxious fumes. Without adequate ventilation, the dust could take hours to settle.

Once the miner was set up for firing he hooked the squibs to battery wires, then unrolled enough wire to allow him to dodge behind a corner pillar. When all was clear, the charge was set off by the battery and the miners then loaded the coal into coal cars set on narrow tracks, which were hooked to a waiting electric engine.

Parsons, at one time, was a thriving little community not unlike many others in those beautiful and endlessly rolling hills. There was a woolen mill, a big tannery, sawmills outside of town, a sand plant, and active coal mines nearby. The churches were full and the money flowed. On Saturday nights there was always a cakewalk in front of the court house. When the music stopped you looked to see if you were standing on the lucky number. If so, you had your pick of a cake the ladies had baked that morning. I never won a cake but I would buy one once in a while, then bring it home to Sarah's folks, pretending how lucky I had been that night at the cakewalk. I never told anyone about buying the cakes. They just couldn't figure it out, I seemed to win all the time. "He's one lucky guy," they'd say. Between us, I think they knew.

I really like that old town of Parsons. Years ago, a story made the rounds. Tucker County's county seat was at that time in the community of St. George, several miles downriver. Parsonites were never happy about that, and they wanted the county seat back. One dark night, a group of determined Parsonites proceeded to St. George and plundered the St. George City Hall. They brought all the deeds, wills, and other records back to Parsons and locked them up for safekeeping. Acquisition by conquest was hardly a democratic thing to do, but it worked.

I have some cemetery lots located high on a hill, overlooking the town. My beloved rivers flow hurriedly by, down below. I always thought it would be nice to know where you were going to be buried. It keeps a person humble. When I stand on my lots, I can see endless towering rolling mountains in all directions. On top of that high hill I get a feeling of space I can't seem to find anywhere else. The cemetery is always full of plastic flowers, mostly roses, which somehow make it through each winter. Fresh batches are placed tenderly in their plastic vases each Memorial Day, and the process is repeated for another year, thoughtfully and inexpensively. I will be hoping for Black-Eyed Susans.

The local politicians do the best they can for their citizens, always ready to embrace the next proposition that might bring state or federal funds.

In August of 1975, I joined Gilbert Gude on his now-famous journey down the 382-mile Potomac River. During this trip, we had a rare look at one of the big drift mines in Bayard, West Virginia. Mines are not generally open to the public; public relations benefits are negligible and the cost to suit-up visitors, disrupt operations, and subject the public to possible safety hazards is not encouraged. Dropping down into a drift mine by mine car is an eerie experience. We were suited in heavy white coveralls and huge black rubber boots, helmeted, and given belts equipped with a few emergency items. Visitors are warned to leave all matches behind. We climbed in the cars and dropped down into the mine at a slant that follows the course (drift) of the coal veins. We had all lost our identities through the look-alike coveralls and the big boots. Every wall is covered with a coating of lime dust, which hardens and keeps coal dust damp to arrest flashing. There isn't a straight line anywhere. There seems to be no escape once you arrive at the bottom of the mine. The miners don't like to be gawked at; noisy machines claw through the coal seams and coal is run out on conveyor belts to the top of the mine. The big claw machines advance to the next veins, which are then chewed through. Every now and then, our guide would take out a short pole and probe the ceiling to be certain it was not about to cave in. Ceilings are fragile and have been known to fall at inopportune times. Women now work in the mines. It has taken a long time for the men to get used to this dramatic change. Superstition had it that if a woman enters a mine it brings bad luck, but the crews we met had adjusted to this interesting fact of life, and it was no longer an issue with either the men or the women.

West Virginians, through the years, have paid a heavy price for the ravaging of their virgin timber lands and the exploitation of the state's vast coal deposits by outsiders. In the early days, miners received little more than slave wages, succumbed to black lung disease, received damaged limbs and death in return for their work. Today abandoned mines discharge sulfuric acid, made up of pyrites, which mix with air and water and foul the river, producing "yellow boy" (ferric sulfate). The "yellow boy" can kill a stream, as in the case of the virtually dead North Branch River. An engineer told me that the only cure is to "let daylight enter the mines, clean 'em, and seal them." As every last vestige of profit is finally wrung out of the land, above and below, it is routinely abandoned. Those who have profited are forced to pay for reclamation and restoration. Most of the folks up here know these things but feel helpless to do anything about them. From a distance, the North Branch Valley is beautiful, but if you look close, it is an environmental shambles.

Unfortunately, in West Virginia and in the upper Potomac Valley, coal is King. There's still about 200 billion tons of coal to be dug out of the hills of the Appalachian highlands. Extracting it may degrade the lovely countryside, but people have to eat and the anxious stockholders expect their dividends. To those who would embrace economics over natural beauty, the mountain vistas are lovely, but one can't eat scenery nor put it in a gas tank. What do most people do about it? They begrudgingly accept it, then go on about their business and think of something else.

HEATERS ISLAND

Virtually all islands in the Potomac are located in Maryland with the exception of those in the District of Columbia. The Maryland boundary extends to the mean low water mark generally on the southerly edge of the river from Smith Point at the river's mouth to Kempton at the Fairfax Stone. For years, larger islands were used for farming, cattle raising, and even for sod, usually of excellent quality. In the early 1960s, a daring entrepreneur planned a country music park on

Heaters Island. (Courtesy of the National Park Service)

Mason Island, which hugs the Virginia shoreline, at the downriver tip of Heaters Island. Nothing came of it. I can only guess the threat of flooding and difficult access put a damper on such plans.

Of the many stories of island life on the Potomac, Heaters Island is one of the most interesting. Heaters Island lies just below the Route 15 bridge at Point of Rocks, Maryland. It is one of a series of large islands lying in the middle of the Potomac River between Point of

Rocks and Great Falls. Heaters comprises about 187 acres of land, and is shaped like a fish, with channels on the Maryland and Virginia sides of near-equal width. It is about 7,500 feet long and 200 feet wide at its center.

All islands in the Potomac suffer the same fate during floods and high freshets: total inundation and scouring. Each island takes on massive amounts of silt, downed trees, and trash at its upper ends during high water. Yet, for many years, Potomac River islands have been used successfully for farming and, although all are now abandoned, these unique river lands can bring high prices when put on the market. The best use of the large islands is for state, county, and private wildlife preserves.

Heaters is of modest size among the Potomac River giants. Just downriver lies Little Mason Island (80 acres), the Big Mason Island (Fair Island), some 300 acres in size, 1 mile above Whites Ferry; Harrison Island (Black Walnut Island), 400 acres; Seldon Island, 400 acres, below Goose Creek; and Seldon's cousin, Van Deventer Island, 50 acres. Watkins Island (about 600 acres) completes the roster of big islands, running 3.5 miles downriver from Seneca Falls to within 2 miles of Great Falls. With the continual erosion of the upper ends of these islands, and the corresponding deposits of soil and flotsam at the downriver ends, these islands are slowly moving downstream, and their acreage changes yearly. Most acreage estimates on Potomac island tax maps are pure conjecture, based on guesses by former owners over the years. Planimetric measurements, based on up-to-date physical boundaries, are certainly more reliable, but there seems little need for such accuracy.

Large islands bring about $1,000 per acre on the open market. Gone are the days of profitable farming or dairying on the islands, due mainly to repeated flooding, high water, and poor access. The 187-acre Heaters Island was sold to the State of Maryland several years ago for $187,000, a solid bench mark for anyone interested in exploring today's Potomac River island real estate market.

Many islands have defective titles, turning out to be breakaway pieces from large tracts along the shorelines, or buildups over the years with no solid clues to their physical origin. Except for some islands that have been farmed, most islands are infested with nettles and poison ivy, providing little in the way of recreation. The bulk of the smaller islands one sees along the river are owned by the State of Maryland and can no longer be purchased or patented.

The National Park Service owns a few islands in the Great Falls area, purchased or donated years ago, but there is presently no authorization to buy land beyond the mean low-water mark, so there have been no islands purchased by the Park Service or others recently. There are occasional privately owned islands, but few are used. The very lovely and historic Sycamore Island Club above Little Falls is an exception.

In 1699, the Piscataway Indians, with their *tayac* (emperor), migrated to an island opposite Point of Rocks, Maryland. *Tayac* is Piscataway for turkey, the Piscataway symbol of authority or leadership. The island (Heaters) was called Conoy Island by the Indians. A settlement was built by the Piscataways on the downriver end of the island. The precise location and remains have been identified by photogrammetry, and there have been a few archaeological excavations here in the past.

Twenty-three years later, in 1722, the Piscataways were on the move. Sadly, most of the tribe had been all but eradicated by smallpox, transmitted by traders' blankets, so fragile was their immunity to the deadly diseases of the Europeans. The few remaining Piscataways left Conoy Island and proceeded to the upper Ohio River area where they joined the Iroquois. In time, even that small portion of the Piscataway tribe vanished.

There are still a few members of the Piscataway tribe surviving in southern Maryland. The last reputed leader of the remaining members of the Piscataway tribe in southern Maryland died several years ago and was buried, appropriately, at Piscataway Park, opposite Mount Vernon, pursuant to special congressional legislation authorizing private burials on government land. This was a fitting tribute to the memory of what was one of the great Indian tribes of the lower Potomac in the early days of the seventeenth century, the days of Captain John Smith and the first Maryland colony at St. Mary's.

Heaters Island was owned by the Heater family who also owned acreage near the community of Furnace Mountain on the Virginia side of the river, not far from Heaters Island. The island was eventually sold to the State of Maryland for its shoreline acquisition program. Heaters Island was used for sod farming in the late 1960s. Every time I float by the island, I take the channel on the Virginia side, which affords access up a bank. I always enjoy poking around where I shouldn't. Access to the island is by "Ford Road" on the Virginia side, half a mile from the top of the island. Ford Road meets a natural ford in the river that was always difficult to scrape over in a canoe in low water. A primitive ferry was installed years ago to accommodate trucks carrying iced lima beans.

In the spring of 1928, the Miskell family moved to the island, staying there until the 1940s, growing corn and wheat, and raising cattle. Jesse Miskell, one of eleven children, filled me in recently on how he survived on Heaters during the Depression years. Jesse's father rented the island from the Heaters. Rent was paid by dividing the Miskell's 80-acre, 800-barrel corn crop each year. Access to the island in those days was by boat or by wading the ford on the Virginia side of the river. In the summer, Jesse would wade across to Point of Rocks or to places along the abandoned C & O Canal where he knew polecats (skunks) could be caught. Jesse would bring the "cats" back to the island and set them free. Before Christmas each year, Jesse would trap them on the island and ship the skins to Sears Roebuck in time to receive his annual Christmas check. With this money he would buy his clothing, shoes, and other essentials for the coming year. He also carried on a lucrative trade in tasty "skunned" catfish.

Jesse tells the story of how his father and his uncle, in 1934, picked up two 40-gallon copper kettles and accompanying coils from the railroad freight station at Point of Rocks. There were no secrets in those days, and it didn't take long for Federal Revenue Agent Cushwa to find out about what seemed to be an illegal enterprise, and before you knew it, Agent Cushwa was circling the island in his boat, looking for evidence. Jesse's father was sitting on the porch when Cushwa arrived, and swore to goodness the copper kettle, coils, and other hardware were not on the island. All the while the copper kettles and coils had been hastily lowered into the cistern with its wooden top in place, no more than an arm's length away from Cushwa's nose. The problem was, part of a coil was sticking out of the water and would have been in full view had Cushwa thought about the cistern as a hiding place and peered down into the water. The agent finally took off and, mercifully, soon all was well. The hardware was now capable of being used to prepare its delectable brew and could be returned to the cistern at any time should a Cushwa alert be sounded.

In mid-March, 1936, a sudden thaw in temperatures from Maryland to the Canadian border led to one of the heaviest floods in the recorded history of the Potomac Valley. The floodwater surpassed all previous high-water marks. Floodwaters fully covered Heaters Island. Before it was over, the depth of the flood was 17 feet for a period of 54 hours.

The floodwaters quickly covered the island and rose fast. The Miskells took to their boat and Jesse's father hung on to the porch with his hands and arms and found himself, later, hanging on to the roof of the house with Jesse holding a lantern between his legs on one of the coldest nights he could remember, March 18, 1936. On the next day, in the late afternoon, the water appeared to recede, and the family, somehow, made its way to higher ground below Point of Rocks.

After the flood, the Miskells took on the awesome task of removing the mud and silt from the house. Thirty-five steers were missing, some weighing in at 1,300 pounds or more. Jesse's father waded the edge of the river on both sides for miles after the flood and managed to recover some of his stock. The Miskells never recovered from that loss, and finally moved off the island in 1942, barely in time to miss yet another vicious Potomac River flood in October of that year.

Farming on Heaters Island was no romantic picnic. Jesse took a job on the railroad, and joyfully returned about nine years ago to his home in Dargan, Maryland, outside of Sharpsburg, after a life full of adventure, hard times, and good luck. Had Jesse's father lost his grip on the house during the flood there would have been no interview with Jesse and his wife, Ethel, on that lovely spring day in Dargan. Ethel wrapped up two pieces of homemade cherry pie for me to take home, complete with one of those melt-in-your mouth crusts. Folks in Dargan sure know how to treat a guy!

Shawnee Canoe Club, Cumberland, Maryland. (Helmer Collection)

THE SHAWNEE CANOE CLUB

There is no better commentary on the cultural life of Cumberland, Maryland, than the story of the Shawnee Canoe Club. At the turn of the century, the nation's canoe clubs became the forerunners of today's country clubs. Every large town or city along a river had one or more, and Cumberland was no exception.

The Shawnee Canoe Club was located in Cumberland, Maryland, on the north side of the North Branch of the Potomac, just up from its confluence with Wills Creek and adjoining the old site of Riverside Park. Both the club and the park are now buried under tons of rip-rap, put in place for the Cumberland-Ridgely flood control project in the 1950s.

Were I to begin my life over again, I would choose to be born in Cumberland, Maryland, just before the close of the nineteenth century so I could become a member of the Shawnee Canoe Club. I would accompany the adventurous members who ranged so far afield in pursuit of their canoe camping fun along the great Potomac and its North and South branches.

In those days, Victorian influences were still felt and manners and dress were still important. Families have always been important in the life of Cumberland and, even today, they are the centerpiece of satisfying daily lives.

The Shawnee Canoe Club was incorporated on February 18, 1897, and organized for pleasure canoeing on the North and South branches of the Potomac River. Cumberland was beginning its finest moments. William McKinley had just been reelected President. A new city hall overlooked Wills Creek. It was built in the French mansard design, well proportioned and impressive. Businesses were bustling and times were good. Cumberland was, as it was called, the Queen City of the Alleghenies. It later became the second largest city in the State of Maryland.

Life must have been fun in those halcyon days. Horseless carriages were available for those who could afford them. It is not surprising that a social and athletic organization like the Shawnee Club was formed. It was made up of prominent and imaginative members and their families who knew how to practice the fine art of having a good time.

Robert Shriver, a prominent Cumberland banker, introduced canoeing to Cumberland. Shriver was the first and only commodore of Cumberland's Shawnee Canoe Club, presiding from 1897 to 1912. In 1881, he purchased his first canoe, made of wood, delicate, handsomely designed and paddled with a double blade. The club canoes were 15 to 16 feet long of the "racine" design, decked, and usually paddled solo with a double blade. Canoes weighed about 75 pounds and could cost as much as $50, a lot of money in those days.

Social events at the club were numerous, especially during the cold months when canoeing was impractical. Card parties, dances, and all manner of other events filled the Shawnee social calendar. In early spring and in the fall, members lounged on the second-story porch to catch the warm sun and observe the comings and goings on the river below the clubhouse. To the east, members could see the guard locks of the old C & O Canal, and hear the bustle of the railroads and the canal basin, one of the grandest scenes in America.

Early canoeing and athletic clubs have always been considered the forerunners of today's country clubs. At the time of the Shawnee

Club, few people could afford a $50 canoe, and working people could not find time or money to engage in sports activities. Six- and even seven-day work weeks were not uncommon.

In the spring and summer, the rivers beckoned. Members' boats were frequently hauled to Dawson, on the North Branch below Keyser, for a day's outing down the North Branch, with a take-out 20 miles below at the Shawnee Clubhouse, a run of five or more hours. River logistics were simple then. Trips on the South Branch required hauling canoes and gear by team and wagon to the put-in at Moorefield or Petersburg. At the conclusion of the South Branch canoe runs at the South Branch and Potomac River confluence, canoes were carried to the nearby C & O Canal and, for a small toll, canoeists simply paddled up-canal, 21 miles to the Shawnee Canoe Club, through six locks and the guard lock at Cumberland. On the other trips, members would load canoes and gear into railroad baggage cars at the end of the day. Trains would stop at South Branch Station, below Oldtown, and return to the center of the city in 30 minutes flat.

Members camped along the way when traveling the rivers. Commodore Shriver knew the landowners along the South Branch as friends and business associates. Landowners frequently enjoyed dinner and campfire fun during periodic Shawnee camp-outs. Shawnee campsites were imaginatively named by club members and recorded on Shriver's 1901 hand-drawn *Map of the South Branch Valley, from Romney to the Potomac,* compiled by members of the Shawnee Canoe Club. Shriver's original map can be found in the Allegany County Historical Society records at "History House" on Washington Street, in Cumberland. One can trace the Shawnee camps from Romney to the North Branch confluence. Among them are Potato Island Camp, Camp Washout, Camp P.D.Q., Willow Beach Camp, Hoophole Camp, Nailhead Camp, Camp Satisfaction, and Cold Lunch Camp.

In June 1904, Robert Shriver, at a youthful 67, Frank Jenvey, William Bruce, and George Daisy embarked on a dangerous river journey down the Potomac, from Cumberland to Washington. There were no reliable maps, and life along the river was primitive and perilous. Each paddled solo with his heavy camping gear. The trip took

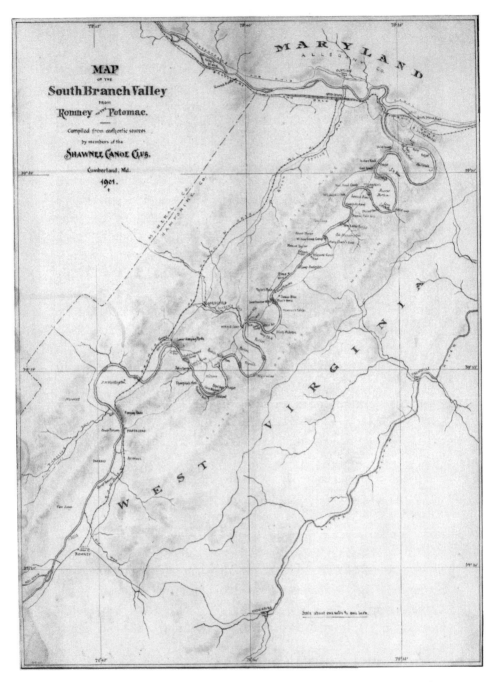

South Branch Valley from Romney to the Potomac, compiled by members of the Shawnee Canoe Club, Cumberland, Maryland, 1901. The original of this map is on file at History House (Allegany County Historical Society) in Cumberland, Maryland. Commodore Robert Shriver penned this map in his unique "banker's script" and it is remarkably accurate.

Four of a kind, Shawnee Canoe Club. (Helmer Collection)

eight days and they finally reached the Great Falls of the Potomac on June 25, 1904. Their spirited pace was due to medium-high water during the trip.

Shriver's Potomac trip had so captured the imagination of the Shawnees that a club trip was organized three months later to Georgetown by passenger canal boat chartered from the Queen City Boat Club. Thirteen members, including their ladies, a young lad, and an infant made up the passenger list. In addition, Captain Baker, an employee of the Queen City Boat Club came with the rental arrangement and was at the rudder, and a mule handler guided the ponderous "luxury liner" to Washington. The passengers stopped to see the canal and surrounding countryside along the way.

Shriver was an expert amateur photographer, having taken up photography at the age of 23 in 1860. He was a pioneer in the cumbersome wet collodion glass negative photographic process. This early equipment was bulky and required prompt development of heavy glass plates, on the spot, as photos were taken. Later, dry-plate glass negatives, precoated and presensitized, were mass produced. Shriver could then take his photographic gear on Shawnee outings and overnight camping trips. Amateurs had to develop and print their own negatives in those days, thus, the success of a photographer was measured by the ability to develop and print. Shriver was the complete photographer and his photos were always well composed. Shriver began to take canoeing pictures as far back as 1898 and his early scenes include some of the most remarkable early canoeing pictures in existence. Much of his early work can be found in the George Eastman House Museum in Rochester, New York. Shriver, "Uncle Bob" to his family and friends, was a bachelor and the third president of Cumberland's First National Bank. Banking, photography, the Shawnee Club, and public service were among Shriver's greatest interests. He was truly one of Cumberland's most revered citizens.

In 1912, Shriver died. With Shriver's enthusiasm and leadership gone and the ominous rumblings of World War I, the Shawnee Club was discontinued and finally disbanded in 1929. Dangerous waves created by motor boats like the *Potomac Queen*, which operated between a dock near the clubhouse and Dreyer's Beach, made canoeing disagreeable and contributed to the demise of the club, but, in the end, it was the loss of Shriver's infectious personality and love of the out-of-doors that was missed and never forgotten. In 1929, the clubhouse was donated to the city for a park as a memorial to their beloved commodore.

Unfortunately, a log of the club's trips cannot be found, but memories of the club's days were elegantly captured through Shriver's lens. We are grateful to him for allowing us to savor a few of yesterday's moments on glass plates and film.

Y-CAMP

Anyone who has been to summer camp will recognize this next story. Y-Camp, just down the road from Springfield, West Virginia, on the South Branch of the Potomac, offered a rare expeience to any boy or girl lucky enough to attend this world of summer magic.

The South Branch of the Potomac River has always been the sum-

Time for a swim at Y-Camp, 1919. (Photo made available by the late Eleanor Holzshu, of Cumberland, Maryland)

mer playground for Cumberland, Maryland, especially in the days when trains, like commuter cars, could whisk families to and from destinations in minutes flat. One wave of the hand and a train would stop and take passenger and baggage to whatever destination was chosen along the route.

There is hardly a Cumberland senior camper or young camper who hasn't visited or heard about Y-Camp summers. Y-Camp was operated by the Cumberland YMCA, and in later years was called Camp Cliffside. It was located just off Route 28 about 2.5 miles below the small town of Springfield, West Virginia. One takes a left turn just before crossing the Route 28 bridge at a most delightful spot called Lower Hanging Rocks, located on the South Branch of the Potomac. The Y-Camp cabins were located on the river on the south side of the bridge. The old bridge that crossed the South Branch here was called Wire Bridge, and was later replaced by Iron Bridge. Today, a modern highway bridge has replaced both.

Often, one's fondest memories of childhood are those of summer camp. The getting ready was sometimes as much fun as the arriving. The memories are almost always sweet. There was something magic about it all . . . and the precious memories will never fade.

The stories of Y-Camp and Camp Cliffside are really stories about the hard work and imagination of two men who, in turn, dedicated their lives to enriching and inspiring the lives of thousands of young men and women. William H. Lewis and Edwin Larrabee Kuhn, affectionately called Uncle Bill and Pappy Kuhn, were responsible for it all. Uncle Bill was the Central YMCA secretary in Cumberland, Maryland, and had been director of Y-Camp since 1914. Uncle Bill retired from the YMCA in 1944, but continued on with the camp, under its new name, Camp Cliffside, as camp director until his death in 1963. Pappy Kuhn joined Uncle Bill in the mid-twenties as YMCA athletic director, and athletic director of Y-Camp. Uncle Bill and Pappy were inseparable, working as a team all their lives. No kinder nor more thoughtful men ever lived.

Uncle Bill quietly contributed to the education of boys and girls by donating part of his salary, and later, his social security earnings, to cover needed tuition and expenses. His caring and devotion to young people and their welfare was the core of his life. Mail was just addressed to Uncle Bill, Frostburg, Maryland, and was always delivered.

Pappy had journeyed from Dixon, Illinois, to join up with Uncle Bill. In Dixon, Pappy had been athletic director at the Dixon YMCA. At Y-Camp, Pappy handled discipline.

The heart of camp life was its daily routine and popular programs. Each day had its similarities: up and at 'em, early; assembly; salute to the flag; a rush to the mess hall for breakfast. After breakfast, the daily routine followed: morning activities, lunch, rest period, afternoon activities, retreat, dinner, campfire, and always a story, then lights out.

Morning and afternoon activities were always special. Boat and canoe trips were favorites with the groups of pirates and buccaneers. Both the pirates and buccaneers would paint their faces, put on funny clothes, and try to sink each other's boats. Mystery trips were also fun: visiting Miller's peach orchards nearby, a visit to the nearby pony farm, or a visit to Hampshire Park in Romney. Once in a while there was time for a visit to Peterkin Episcopal Church Camp for a day's outing. A totally unreliable truck was usually on hand to transport the campers. The return to camp in the truck was always noisy.

One favorite subject at the evening campfire was to tell the story of the ghost of John Blue who was supposed to have been killed for his gold by his handyman. John Blue would always appear when there was a full moon and begin looking for his gold. As the horror story came to an end, there was a scuffling on top of the hill overlooking the campfire. After much muttering and moaning, the ghost of John Blue weaved down the path, swinging his rusty dark lantern to and fro as he continued to search for his gold. John Blue came nearer and nearer. First-time campers trembled and then froze. Those who were in on the fun would let out blood-curdling screams and the first-timers ran for their lives, hiding inside the tents and under their cots. One can hardly imagine how many times the story of old John Blue and his gold was recounted when the campers returned home.

Stunt nights are still fondly recalled by the old campers. Each tent or cabin would provide humorous skits and compete for the first prize. A highlight and privilege for campers was an opportunity to ride the truck into Springfield, West Virginia, daily, to pick up the mail and needed supplies. Campers kept their money on deposit with the camp store, drawing it out in pennies after rest period for a piece of candy or other treats.

Mr. and Mrs. Charles J. Blue, the owners of the surrounding lands, rented the camp to the Cumberland YMCA. A handshake agreement was enough. Campers arrived by car, truck, or train. It took 45 minutes from Cumberland to the drop off, a mile from the camp. The train tracks are still used today, and run from Green Spring, West Virginia, across the river from Oldtown, Maryland, to Petersburg, West Virginia. The train stopped at a point called Gracie Station at an old mill site. Campers would disembark and somehow get their gear to camp, a mile away. There were always creative ways to transport camp gear: by horse, wheelbarrow, by truck, which seldom worked, or by just plain carrying, both ways. Boys and girls from 7 to 15 years were accepted for camp. The average stay for boy's camp was four weeks, and two to three weeks for the alternating girl's camp.

The South Branch offered good swimming down from the bridge. Nonswimmers hovered around Pappy's "small dock" until they could convince Pappy they could swim, then they were entitled to enjoy the deeper water, the sliding boards, and the diving board at the "big dock." The ultimate test required a swim from the Y-Camp beach to John Blue's beach across the river and return. The "Big Dockers" gained status, and could now hover around the boat dock and use the canoes due to their swimming prowess.

When Y-Camp started in 1914, fees were $4.00 a week, increasing to $40 to $50 a week by 1969 when Cliffside closed. Times had been changing, and county health standards became so stringent that group camps like Y-Camp and Cliffside found it impossible to operate. Even the icy cold and delicious spring water coming downhill from the camp waterpipe was looked upon with suspicion by the county health sleuths. Portable toilets, no matter how well maintained, were thumbs down as far as the county was concerned. The enchanted way of the small and rustic boys' and girls' camp was coming to an end.

Uncle Bill retired from the Cumberland Y in 1944 and immediately moved to Camp Cliffside, same camp, same location, just renamed, this time run by James R. "Jim" Lemmert and his brother, Howard H. "Howie" Lemmert. Louise Hanson Lemmert, mother of Jim and Howard, was an assistant chaperon. Dr. Tim Lewis, one of Cumberland's top surgeons, stayed with the camp for many years, as did C. A. "Soupy" Lancaster, managing editor of Cumberland's *Evening* and *Sunday Times*. Both Tim Lewis and Soupy had attended the Y-Camp summer sessions for years when they were kids. Dr. Lewis was a nephew of Uncle Bill's, the great uncle of Jim and Howard Lemmert, and the "real uncle" of Mrs. Louise Hanson Lemmert, now 85 years young and living in Frostburg. Nearby neighbors, the James Wrights, the Matlicks, and the Whites, were helpful in assisting with the restoration of the camp after major floods damaged the camp buildings in 1950 and 1954.

With the close of Y-Camp in 1944 and Cliffside in 1969, it became clear that both camps had served a grateful and eager public for 55 fulfilling years, during which time thousands of boys and girls heard the macabre story of John Blue's stolen gold. It was at the camp that the boys and girls received inspiration, love, and caring from the hard-working and dedicated counselors who made the unique programs and activities of the two camps so successful. Toward the end, senior campers still relived the golden days of the camps by checking into Alumni Hall, a cabin set aside for those who wished to join in the fun and be young just one more time.

Uncle Bill died in June 1963 while still in camp residence. He was always fit, and looked handsome and youthful. Pappy Kuhn also moved to Camp Cliffside upon his retirement, building a small cabin on the grounds back in the woods where he would live out the rest of his busy life. He passed on in the 1970s. The 1985 flood stripped 2 acres of land from the campground. Cabins and about half the trees were lost at the camp. I know the warm memories so many have of that hallowed piece of ground along the river.

Mrs. Blue sent the Lemmerts a postcard a number of years ago, offering to sell them the camp. The deal was made and the camp is now owned by those who love it most. Jim and Howard and their families spend a lot of time reminiscing with their friends at the camp. One of their friends is me, I am proud to say.

Chapter 8.

A PARK IS BORN

In September 1938, almost 100 years after the ceremony marking its opening, the United States acquired the 184½-mile derelict C & O Canal from the Baltimore and Ohio Railroad for $2 million. Historic restoration was begun on the lower 22 miles of the canal from Violettes Lock to Georgetown. On George Washington's birthday, the following year, the canal was appropriately dedicated as a public park, marking the beginning of a 50-year struggle by conservation groups and the general public to turn the old ditch into the kind of park it deserved to be. After all, was it not the oldest intact nineteenth-century canal in America? Its pedigree was impeccable with historical ties to George Washington, Thomas Jefferson, and James Madison. But new days were not to dawn just yet. A ruinous flood in 1942 and a World War diverted all interest away from the canal, and it continued to lie dormant for almost 30 years more before it gained national historical park status.

During this hiatus, two major attitudes toward the canal emerged: the first was the outlook of those who viewed the canal as a musty relic of the past that could be turned into a tourist attraction by building a roadway at the edge of the river above Great Falls, Maryland, to Cumberland, Maryland, 169 miles upstream. In the 1950s,

Remains of the upper and lower lock gates on the C & O Canal. (Photo by M. Woodbridge Williams, National Park Service)

Cumberland was in the midst of an economic decline, and saw the parkway proposal as a means of drawing tourists with cash in their pockets, bringing new jobs. There was also much interest and support in Washington to build a parkway along the narrow canal route as a means of expanding traffic capacity throughout the nation's capital and the city of Cumberland. Washingtonians knew little about what the river or canal looked like above the city, nor did they seem to care. There was no visible or vocal constituency for a recreational canal and towpath as we know it today.

The second attitude toward the canal could be discerned in the new breed of conservationists that was emerging in all parts of the nation, and especially in Washington, D.C. These people were politically astute and unyielding. World War II was over, and it was time to direct the public's attention to the new environmental ethic. It was the beginning of the era of Rachel Carson and others who warned us about the effects of the poisons that kill and stunt and the relationship between all living organisms and their environment.

The politicians wanted to seize the moment and pave over this rare example of an unaltered nineteenth-century trade route and build a parkway in the flood plain, on fragile soils deposited by floods, along with a two-lane road that would become outdated before it was finished. On August 16, 1950, Assistant Secretary of the Interior Dale E. Doty, espousing the party line, threw his "Chesapeake and Ohio Canal Report" on the table.

The report had just been transmitted to Speaker of the House of Representatives Sam Rayburn. It was a joint survey prepared by the Bureau of Public Roads of the Department of Commerce and the National Park Service. The report boasted: "It is practicable to construct a parkway along this canal and it is advisable to do so, provided additional right-of-way can be obtained." The 87-page document came with eight pullouts and a face sheet entitled, "Proposed C & O Canal Parkway." The plan was for a Blue Ridge/Skyline Drive highway along the Potomac River's edge, from Great Falls to Cumberland, Maryland, providing automobile access to the canal's best-preserved historic and scenic attractions. The joint survey described the scenic character of the river and the canal in eloquent terms: "unchanged by the passage of time, a winding, twisting river, plunging over numerous rapids and falls through narrow gorges, and flowing through quiet pools in fertile valleys, amid scenes as widely contrasting as those of bucolic tranquility and primordial rock formations."

The survey even used Thomas Jefferson to sell the parkway proposal. A quote from Jefferson when he had looked upon the passage of the Potomac through the Blue Ridge at Harpers Ferry Gap was incorporated in the report: "It is a true contrast to the foreground. It is as placid and delightful as wild and tremendous. For the mountain being cloven asunder, she presents to your eye through the cleft a small catch of blue, a horizon at an infinite distance in the plain country, inviting you as it were from the riot and turmoil roaring around to pass through the breach to calm below." This description ended with Jefferson's folksy, but time-worn old saw, "This scene is worth a voyage across the Atlantic." The joint survey was seemingly a tourist folder, a masterpiece of joyous adjectives, blue skies, and happy days. It estimated an automobile traffic volume of 8,500 vehicles per day for the section between Great Falls and Point of Rocks, a distance of 33 miles. This innocent statistic reminds us of how pleasant life was in 1950.

Seven initial development areas were selected from Great Falls to Cumberland. The parkway pavement would be 24-feet wide with 8-foot shoulders throughout. The pavement would consist of a course of 2 inches of asphaltic concrete on a 9-inch crushed stone or gravel base. The existing federal land ownership of 28 acres per mile would be increased to at least 100 acres per mile. Land costs were explained by simply observing that the State of Maryland would probably be interested in providing funds for this purpose. The Paw Paw Tunnel could be used for parkway construction, but the tunnel towpath would have to be ripped out. Parkway costs, in 1950 dollars, were $17 million, including canal restoration. A closer look at potential flood restoration costs might well have reversed the hearty recommendations and saved everyone a lot of time and money. Yet the matter of potential flood damages was discussed in the survey report with the observation that "Potomac River floods do not render the construction of a parkway either impractical or inadvisable." Flooding was treated as an infrequent nuisance, "accordingly it is concluded that interruption of traffic due to occasional floods along the canal would be of no importance, and that injury to the parkway itself by such floods would not be serious." Secretary of the Interior Douglas McKay's imprimatur was nowhere to be seen on the document, but he did not hesitate to fully endorse the proposal, compelling the National Park Service not only to fall in line, but to assist in writing the "happy" but totally misleading joint survey recommendations. The old canal as a priceless historic resource appeared to be dead in the water. The parkway was seemingly about to become a reality.

In defense of the parkway supporters, the proposal should be looked upon within the context of the times. Parkways were popular. The Blue Ridge Parkway and Skyline Drive were classic park roadways and enjoyed wide approval. The nation had just "won" a World War, apparently almost single-handedly, at least so it seemed to the American public, and a "can-do" attitude prevailed. After all, hadn't we built airstrips on remote islands in the Pacific? Hadn't we welded together ships, airplanes, and tanks by the hundreds? So what's the fuss about building a 169-mile highway along the river from Great Falls? If the floods wreck it, we'll just push the debris in the river and build the thing all over again, bigger and better. It's not as if we had a money problem! Such seemed to be the attitude of many Americans regarding the parkway scheme.

In 1950, five years after World War II, hiking and biking as we know it today had not become popular. These were still the squad-tent and folding-cot days. The army surplus stores were the nation's outfitters. Light packs, freeze-dried foods, and self-inflating air mat-tresses were unheard of. Public land was supposed to be used for construction and development, and yes, even for parkways. The idea of the Park Service acquiring land just to look at was misunderstood. There was not the widespread longing for vast open spaces with its solitude and inspiration. At least a parkway would insure that the old ditch would be used for more than bird-watching and scout hikes.

Soon, a nationwide love affair with the outdoors began and a sleeping giant awoke. The Appalachian Trail was rediscovered, and those who had canoes packed it all amidships and shoved off for ad-ventures in far-away places. The outside world was to be enjoyed, but something had to be done with that derelict old canal. The re-sponse was pave it over and be quick about it!

What was really needed was someone tough enough to take on the Department of the Interior, the politicians, and even the President, if need be. There was an urgent need for a bull-by-the-horns kind of conservationist. The right man at the right time stepped forward, William Orville Douglas, an associate justice of the Supreme Court, tough outdoorsman, mountain climber, and indefatigable canal hiker. Douglas had spent a lot of time walking the towpath near his home in Washington, and knew the value of this enchanted byway. He also knew the canal was in serious trouble and that it was time for action. He described the park as a "refuge, a place of retreat, a long stretch of quiet and peace at the Capital's back door . . . a wilderness area where one can commune with God and with nature. A place not yet marred by the roar of wheels and the sound of horns."

Douglas believed that the outdoors was a cure for many walking troubles. He had faith in walking and the mountains. This philosophy is found in his writings. He credits walking in the hills and mountains near his early home in Yakima Valley, Oregon, with curing his polio as a young boy. He could see the benefits of conservation; he had seen his beloved West denuded of trees and suffering from soil erosion. Saving the canal from parkway proponents was possible he thought, and he entered the fray determined to win.

Luck and providence came to the rescue of the C & O Canal when it was least expected. The events that follow have affected more people than we will ever know. Justice Douglas seized his opportunity. Merlo J. Pusey wrote an editorial for the *Washington Post* on January 3, 1954, agreeing with the recommendations of the joint survey: constructing a parkway from Great Falls to Cumberland along the C & O Canal. Two weeks later, Douglas, in a letter to the editor, challenged the editorial writer:

I wish the man who wrote your editorial of January 3, 1954, approving the Parkway, would take time off and come with me. We would go with packs on our backs and walk the 185 miles to Cumberland. I feel that if your editor did, he would return a new man and use the power of your great editorial page to help keep this sanctuary untouched.

Douglas's unique challenge was eagerly accepted by Pusey and Robert H. Estabrook, chief of the *Washington Post* editorial page. In an editorial entitled "We Accept," the editors concluded with: "We are sufficiently enthusiastic about it to wear some blisters on our feet, but we do not believe this back-yard wilderness so near to Washington should be kept closed to those who cannot hike 15 or 20 miles a day."

The *Post* reasoned that the parkway proposal would make the park more accessible. Although most of the conservationists agreed in principle, the questions always remained: What kind of road? How big? Where would it be located? No one could furnish specifics. These questions were at the heart of the issue. It was Justice Douglas's idea to prove that the parkway must not be built near the historic canal, and that the original canal must be left in its natural state.

Requests to join the trip poured in, and the original plan to have only Justice Douglas and the two newspapermen hike the distance by themselves was now out of the question. Interest began to expand out of control. With the growing attention, Douglas reasoned that it might be a good idea to round up the cream of the conservation elite to march with him to articulate his arguments. Among the more illustrious conservationists and canal supporters was the late Anthony Wayne Smith, who, along with Justice Douglas, could use his unique brand of political savvy to nail down his position. Without the leadership and unusual talents of these men, the endeavor would not have withstood the unyielding pressures from so many entrenched politicians and their supporting casts.

At first the hike was planned to begin in Washington and end in Cumberland, but the gallants unanimously decided it would be easier to walk 184 miles downhill from Cumberland. They could also expect to enjoy a huge bite of free publicity as the hikers leisurely strolled into Washington, vigorous and fit, for all to see. By the time the party reached Cumberland, two dozen eager hikers were ready to hit the towpath and head for Washington with packs on their backs, as Douglas had suggested.

Douglas's plan was simple: he would invite hiking companions from the conservation community and the press. Through the media of radio and television he would share the controversy with the public, and extol his views. At the end of the hike he would write a letter to Secretary McKay, setting forth his recommendations. He knew before the hike that he wanted the historic canal restored and left intact to preserve its natural values. He would hike the canal from Cumberland to Georgetown in eight days—no small endeavor—averaging 21 miles a day. This hell-for-leather hiker was determined to walk the canal park into existence from beginning to end.

On the afternoon of March 19, 1954, the party left Washington's Union Station, traveling in a special Baltimore and Ohio observation car attached to the *Chicago Express*. Upon arriving in Cumberland, Maryland, the car was placed on a siding while Senator J. Glenn Beall and other notables welcomed the group. A huge banquet was held at the Cumberland Country Club, with welcoming speeches spiced with "for and against" remarks on the parkway proposal. It was a gathering of great enthusiasm and good cheer; each party attempted to influence the other with impressive orations and their respective perceptions of sound reasoning.

The hike began the next day at Blue Spring, Lock 72, on the canal, a few miles downriver from Cumberland. The events leading up to the Douglas hike captured regional and national attention and drew the curious at local points along the way. One landowner living along the canal saw to it that the trees between the towpath and the river were properly whitewashed, an old canal custom of yesteryear that kept mule handler and mule from blundering into the unyielding sycamores at night.

Potomac Valley sporting clubs rallied, providing meals and shelter; the Appalachian Trail Club filled in as needed. President of the club, Fred Blackburn, and members Bill Schorr, Glenn Skaggs, Bill Mensch, Bill Richardson, and Charlie Thomas, all tough campaigners, cooked the food and washed the dishes when the party wasn't being wined and dined by the eager sporting clubs along the trail.

Magazines and the big wire services publicized the event as it progressed toward Washington. Among the conservation notables were Olaus Murie, president of the Wilderness Society; Sigurd Olson, outdoorsman and president of the National Parks Association; geologist Bill Davies; Dr. Irston Barnes, president of the Audubon Society of the District of Columbia; and Dr. Walter S. Sanderlin, professor and author of many canal books and articles. Park Service Chief Naturalist Drew Chick joined in, and Abbie Rowe was the official hike photographer. Members of national and international conservation groups joined to learn more about Justice Douglas's views.

Local townsfolk greeted the hikers as they made their way past the very towns that had been so much a part of the old canal during its operation. Schools were dismissed, and students swarmed around Douglas and his hiking companions for autographs. The hiking justice was beseeched to take care of a host of tough local matters, including problems with buzzards and mosquitos. The hikers were met with baskets of apples, sandwiches, and cookies, while the onlookers cheered Douglas's worthy cause. "Save the Canal from the National Park Service!" was the cry heard daily along the towpath.

The media coverage was everything the parkway opponents could have hoped for. Newsreels and television updated the event every evening. The hike and its message had captured the imagination of

The Immortal Nine. (Courtesy of the National Park Service)

the public. Indeed, the Douglas hike was to become legendary. It is still the inspiration of the ever-growing C & O Canal Association in Washington. Some people, with tongue in cheek, called the event "The Holy Pilgrimage," and indeed it was!

On the eighth and final day, nine of the original hikers were still at it. Twenty-eight other hikers joined in, but the nine originals persevered to the end, blisters and all. The nine dubbed themselves "The Immortal Nine." For the history books, the nine who walked the entire length of the canal were Grant Conway, Olaus J. Murie, Jack Pearmain, Colin Ritter, Albert E. Farwell, William O. Douglas, Harvey Broome, George Frederick Miller, and Constant Southworth.

Details and events of the hike were celebrated by making up delightfully rowdy verses to the hikers' "C & O Canal Song," which subsequently ended up with a total of 31 "authorized" stanzas by the time the group reached Georgetown. Interior Secretary McKay met Justice Douglas and his stalwarts on the towpath at Lock 6 as they marched to the finish. When the group reached Lock 5, 4 miles from the end of the journey, the hikers boarded a park canal boat. "Little Scat" Eaton guided the canal boat with its honored freight to the tie-up below Thomas Jefferson Street. "Little Scat" was the son of "Big Scat." The two "Scats" had guided the last canal boat into Cumberland before the canal closed down in 1924.

The hikers sang out the last two verses of their C & O Canal song:

> The blisters are a'burnin'
> And the tendon's getting sore,
> While the shutter-boys from Washington
> Keep yelling "Just one more!"

> And now our journey's ended,
> Our aches and troubles gone;
> But blisters heal, so says the *Post*
> And memories linger on.

The hike was over.

On April 22, Supreme Court Associate Justice William O. Douglas forwarded the recommendations of his C & O Canal Committee to Secretary of the Interior Douglas McKay. There were four general recommendations: the canal should be preserved as a recreational entity; the canal should remain as a unit of the park system, bearing some historic name with a budget adequate for its maintenance and supervision; the canal should be developed as a recreation area; and a parkway system should be constructed from Cumberland to Washington, but not on the canal proper. The editors from the *Washington Post* conceded that the canal should be preserved, but asserted that some compromise should be sought to provide for automobile access to the park's natural and historic attractions.

Secretary McKay, in his May 4, 1954, response to Justice Douglas's recommendations, managed to keep the controversy alive and well through a disappointing but polite response. McKay noted that the suggestions by the C & O Canal Committee closely paralleled those of the Department of Interior, and that there was complete agreement on the major objectives to be achieved. "Interior's plans were quite preliminary," he went on to say, "and must be kept flexible and imaginative enough to recognize all of the scenic and historic potentials of the river valley." Finally, "Ideas developed by the C & O Canal Committee will have the fullest possible consideration." It was obvious by this couched and labored reply that McKay received the

Associate Justice William O. Douglas and Secretary of the Interior Stewart L. Udall on the towpath, 1965. (Photo by Nicholas Dean)

biggest jolt of his political career when he discovered the extent of public sentiment in favor of keeping the canal intact and scrapping the parkway idea.

Through the newspapers, radio, and television, Douglas's constituency grew enormously those eight days. For the first time, public attention was riveted on the C & O Canal as an expression of natural and historic values, not as a vehicular parkway. Communities in the valley, hikers, canoeists, farmers, and politicians all got a good glimpse of the "furriners" who had traveled so far up-canal to narrow the controversy. Local people had hoped the proposal would go away some day, but felt powerless to do anything about it. In their estimation, it was simply another case of politicians making decisions to build roads in other people's backyards.

Had it not been for William O. Douglas, the park would have certainly become the proverbial giraffe designed by a committee.

Through political compromise, some sort of natural park might have evolved that would have included the intrusions of growing vehicular access roads, endangering the park's fragile environment.

But the controversy is still not over. There are many people in the towns and living along the river who will always choose short-term benefits rather than long-term values of preservation for future generations. There are those along the C & O Canal who still remember the sting of Justice Douglas's persuasive environmental ethic. There are also those who still think the canal should be turned into a riverside highway to help their local economies "bring tourists to the canal."

There was still some unfinished business. First, there was a plan to designate the old ditch as an historical park. Second, additional land was needed to supplement the 5,257 acres making up the existing park, to meet the standards for such a coveted role in the nation's park system. Before it was over, politicians squirmed, landowners were forced to sell, and the final development plan, presented to and approved by the Congress, was scrapped in favor of the park's advisory commission plan. This latter plan was indeed a giraffe of sorts, but one that the majority of the public endorsed and that will likely be supported for a long time to come.

The groundswell of support for C & O Canal Park status continued. The Canal Committee continued to hold meetings, and Douglas instituted periodic weekend hikes to keep up the tempo. McKay's tenure as Secretary of the Interior ended in 1956. His successor, Fred A. Seaton, showed little interest in resurrecting the parkway issue.

On January 23, 1961, at a late hour, just before John F. Kennedy was to be sworn in as President of the United States, President Dwight Eisenhower signed Presidential Proclamation 3391, establishing the Chesapeake and Ohio Canal National Monument in Maryland. The monument included 4,800 acres of the existing 5,257-acre park from Cumberland to a location 100 feet downstream from the first culvert above the Seneca aqueduct. The proclamation contained familiar language, designed to warm the hearts of all military engineers:

Nothing in this Proclamation is intended to prejudice the use of the Chesapeake and Ohio National Monument for such works as the Congress may hereafter authorize for municipal and domestic water supply, navigation, flood control, drainage, recreation, or other beneficial purposes.

The proclamation was less than meaningless. It conferred no status or authorization for the canal. To the contrary, it provided that the U.S. Army Corps of Engineers continue its relentless push to implement its solution to the region's water and flushing problems: sixteen major multipurpose reservoirs on the Potomac and its tributaries, a permanent revision of free-flowing stream system concepts that would inundate the canal for miles and cause the accompanying loss of thousands upon thousands of acres of productive land. This was a grave moment for those who had worked so hard to save the canal and the valley from senseless oblivion. To its credit, however, the Corps began listening to the uproar of the public and Congress and began curtailing many of its more extensive planning proposals.

In his 1965 State of the Union message and at a time when all park proposals had hit bottom, President Lyndon Johnson announced, upon the advice of Interior Secretary Stewart L. Udall, that a new study be undertaken on the Potomac and that "The river rich in history and memory which flows by our Nation's Capital should serve as a model of scenic and recreation values for the entire country." Udall, following Johnson's lead, saw to it that the study was conducted, that the Army Corps and the District of Columbia engineers were eclipsed, and that all study of the Corps' massive River Bend Dam proposal, especially, was shelved.

A federal Interdepartmental Task Force was set up under the able chairmanship of Kenneth Holum. Planners and all manner of professionals began taking inventory of the basin's natural, cultural, and recreational assets. It was an exercise that included the thoughts and ideas of the adjoining states and the District of Columbia as well as selected federal government disciplines.

In addition, to insure that there would be no fragmented approaches to the planning process, Udall invited the American Institute of Architects to appoint a Potomac Planning Task Force to study ways and means to carry out President Johnson's directive to "clean up the river and keep it clean, to protect its natural beauties and provide for adequate recreational facilities." Appointees to the task force were imaginative architects and scholars such as Grady Clay of Louisville, Kentucky; Frederick Gutheim and Francis Lethbridge of the Washington, D.C. area; Ian L. McHarg of Philadelphia; and others.

Secretary Udall was personally involved in every facet of Potomac National River planning, braving hostile audiences and hard questions from the Congress. I was privileged to make my contributions to the task force plan, and somehow knew it would fly. Others were skeptical. The National Park System was experiencing an expansion of its public holdings beyond the wildest dreams of even its most ardent supporters. The Land and Water Conservation Fund had let loose an avalanche of land acquisition money sufficient to acquire some 80 new parks before the faucet was turned off in the early 1970s. Some phrased it, "acquiring the best of what's left in America." Certainly the Potomac National River would now become a reality.

The public was convinced that the May 1966 Potomac Sub-Task Force report was "the plan" for the National River with its vast "take" areas miles long and miles wide. The document was indeed impressive, 20 inches wide and 80 pages long, with page after page of reasons why immense areas of open space, transportation corridors, and more, should be discussed among federal, state, and local agencies and citizen's groups so that specifics could be presented to President Johnson in less than six months. The public was convinced that they were looking at Interior's "take-no-prisoners" plan to ravage every square inch of countryside from Cumberland to Point Lookout. In their hands was "the plan" for the Potomac National River, a planner's tour de force, the largest land-grab the nation would ever see. The report was not viewed as a joint action to "save" the valley, but a crass "takeover" by the feds. The plan emphasized that without strong land-use controls, the southern boundary of the Potomac was headed for oblivion.

Although well-meaning, the plan seemingly sounded the death knell for any future consideration of Potomac River recreational planning on the West Virginia shore. The task force report was not viewed as an invitation for joint action. West Virginians were convinced that the state's very sovereignty was at stake. "Keep them lands guys outa here" was their cry. West Virginians don't like to be told what to do; their state motto *"Montani semper liberi"* aptly reflects this attitude.

Supporters of the canal park proposal began to grumble that the Potomac National River proposal, which now included the C & O Canal, was too big a chunk to swallow. Further, they feared that the canal park would sink under the weight of the national river plan. They wanted the C & O Canal legislation badly, but not if the Potomac National River plan would eclipse it. The matter was finally settled by Wayne N. Aspinall of Colorado, chairman of the House Committee on Interior and Insular Affairs. The total proposal was too big and too expensive for Aspinall's liking, so hearings would be held only on the canal portion. The great moment began with a hearing before Chairman Roy A. Taylor's Subcommittee on National Parks and Recreation of six different House bills. The Canal legislation (PL 91-664) was finally approved on January 8, 1971.

Senator Charles McCMathias of Maryland introduced a Senate bill similar to the House bill, and it was passed December 22, 1970. The act to establish and develop the Chesapeake and Ohio Canal National Historical Park was approved and signed by President Richard M. Nixon on January 8, 1971. And so, 33 years after the B & O Railroad transferred all right, title, and interest in the canal to the United States, the old ditch had, at last, become a national historical park.

The proposal went far beyond the wildest dreams of canal enthusiasts. The park would be expanded from 5,257 acres to 20,239 acres, with $17 million in development money (1970 prices). The Christmas tree would have more on its outstretched branches: parking areas, comfort stations, interpretive shelters, maintenance buildings, restorations of locks, lockhouses, and the towpath. There would be marinas, picnic areas, bridle trails, roads, environmental education centers, and more. The hard-core constituency, mostly yesteryear's fighters, weary and numb, wanted no part of environmental centers, marinas, and the like. They felt the new plan was, in some respects, almost as bad as the parkway proposal. What had happened was obvious: the Park Service planners had simply taken the canal portion of the national river proposal and turned it into the C & O Canal National Historical Park, which in turn had been rushed through the

The Canal Clipper on its way to Washington. (Courtesy of the National Park Service)

hearing process and approved. But, in all, the park supporters were joyous. They had devised a secret plan to deal with the marinas and the other warts on their revision list.

The legislation called for a 19-member advisory commission, not uncommon for new and emerging parks. Nancy Long of Glen Echo, Maryland, was chosen as first chairperson. The commission's first meeting was held in Secretary Roger C. B. Morton's office on December 20, 1971. Quite often, citizen advisory commissions tend to be at their best toward the beginning of their responsibilities, but this one proved not be the case and is to be congratulated for its four long years of hard work in hammering out one of the best linear park plans in the National Park Service.

Justice William O. Douglas was appointed C & O Canal commission advisor. His fervent hope was that the aqueducts be repaired to insure through-hiking on the towpath from Georgetown to Cumberland. Sitting on that commission seemed to be truly a golden moment for the Justice, and I was privileged to see the light shining in his rugged and handsome face that day when he was sworn in with the other advisory commission members.

What was needed without delay was a low-key and sensitive plan, without intrusive developments: a restrained plan that would preserve the canal and the remains of its historic fabric. The matters of planned overdevelopment, marinas, and other intrusions on the historic park were thrown on the table. The park planners took a beating. I have often thought, "first, we had a swearing in and then we had a swearing at," but it was for the most part constructive criticism. The commission took matters into its own hands, holding many public meetings in towns along the river to work out differences. The plan took four years to complete and it is still on the books, intact and thriving after 17 years. And thus, a park was born.

Chapter 9.

THE RIVER RUNNETH OVER

Major floods in the Potomac Valley are caused by a variety of unpredictable and capricious weather events that are sometimes initiated thousands of miles away. Seedling storms, formed in the Caribbean, the south and Mid-Atlantic oceans, and as far away as the coasts of Africa, set their courses for the Gulf and Atlantic coasts, and grow in intensity as they approach our warm Gulf waters before they slam into the U.S. mainland. Here they begin their orgies of reckless destruction. Each year, some 100 storms of varying strengths develop. Ten or more reach tropical storm intensities; four or five reach full hurricane force.

There have been 28 major Potomac River floods in the past 161 years, but only six great floods in the past 100 or so years, causing one to be skeptical about the continued loose references to "100-year floods." Flooding rains can occur anytime; long-range weather predications are pure guesswork. The 28 major Potomac River floods do not include near-floods, freshets, or ice freshets, also called "ice gorges" or "ice jams," which occur when the river is frozen and the pressures beneath the ice cause surface buckling. Thick irregular masses of ice break off from the ice sheets, making their way downriver, sometimes causing massive pileups. The ice-blocks are pushed up the river banks and chew into tree trunks, gouging deep oval-shaped scars into the bark of any tree that stands in the way. These gouges seldom heal. Severely bruised trees from ice freshets can die off in a couple of years. Potomac floods are also caused by fierce local storms, some with accompanying flash flooding, inflicting sudden devastation. Melting ice over vast land areas can also trigger insidiously quick rises in water levels. Here is my selection of the six most severe Potomac River floods since 1889.

THE FLOOD OF 1889

This Potomac River flood is sometimes linked with the infamous Johnstown Flood as the rains in the Potomac were the same devastating rains that fell in Johnstown, Pennsylvania. At its peak, the Potomac rose 2.8 feet above the Baltimore and Ohio rails on the Harpers Ferry Bridge. Just below Harpers Ferry at Sandy Hook, the water reached a point 8 feet higher than the railroad tracks, which were 17 feet above the canal itself.

In 1889 there were no sea walls or flood protection levees along the banks of the Potomac River. Consequently, the floodwaters rushed into Washington, inundating Pennsylvania Avenue and other nearby low-lying areas. Canal boats from the beleaguered canal broke loose and floated free, beginning their long journeys down the Potomac, eventually crashing into the old Long Bridge (14th Street Bridge) on their way downriver. A train of loaded freight cars was backed onto the Long Bridge to hold it down. With such heavy ballast, the bridge withstood the additional shocks of floating buildings and large trees. The flood waters also carried away mule teams, and destroyed over 170 canal boats and their cargoes. Fish were caught on Pennsylvania Avenue.

This was the flood that sent the C & O Canal into receivership. The B & O Railroad gained control of the canal, emerging as the majority owner of both its 1844 and 1878 bonds, giving it ownership of the preferred mortgages on the physical property, and the right to all canal revenues. It was, in effect, the end of the canal era. The canal was repaired by the railroad at great expense. It began to build its

own canal boats and hire captains and crews. In time, few independent captains were still in business.

THE FLOOD OF MARCH 29, 1924

This was the first major flood in 35 years. It completely wrecked the
C & O Canal. The flood was caused by melting snow and heavy
rains. Valley newspaper editorials, for the first time, put the blame on
heavy timber-cutting in the Allegheny Mountain watershed. Cumberland, the worst hit town on the river, suffered property losses in excess of $3 million. The canal shut down permanently as a conse-
quence of this flood. The flood surpassed all previous high-water
records with a crest in Georgetown 7 inches higher than that of the
1889 flood.

THE FLOOD OF MARCH 18, 1936

Flood waters from the North Branch of the Potomac, and Wills
Creek at Cumberland, carried telephone poles, automobiles, and anything else that lay in the way. Sudden thawing in the winter temperatures throughout the eastern United States from Maryland to the
Canadian border in mid-March 1936, caused the heaviest flood in
the recorded history of the Potomac Valley. In Georgetown, the 1936
crest was higher than it had been in the 1889 flood.

This is the flood that washed all the farms off the mountains in the
Smokehole region of the South Branch of the Potomac above Petersburg. The farmers lost everything, including their way of life. Few
ever returned. The next day, March 19, in Washington, the crest of
the flood was reached. Had the water not been diverted by a levee,
hastily constructed of sand bags placed across the Mall, the floodwaters would have poured into the Federal Triangle. I was living in
Washington near the river at the time, and together with my mother
and our neighbors, watched the turbulent brown water hissing past
the Lincoln Memorial, carrying pieces of houses and bridges in its
grip. The Lincoln Memorial was eerily resting on what resembled an
island, surrounded by water. A freight schooner was stranded near
the Washington Monument grounds. This flood has been called "The

Record Flood" by people in the Potomac Valley. No flood before or after 1936 has matched its velocity and destructive power, particularly at the head of the South Branch Valley. This is the flood old timers in the valley still talk about. Both the Harpers Ferry and Shepherdstown bridges were washed out. The bridge at Williamsport was the only bridge still standing above Washington when the flood waters subsided. The 1936 flood is frequently used as a benchmark to measure subsequent flood levels. Some have come close, but "The Record Flood" has yet to be surpassed, particularly in the upper valley.

THE FLOOD OF OCTOBER 15–17, 1942

The Potomac again went over its banks. This flood put the C & O Canal back into the wrecked condition the United States government found it in in 1938 when it was acquired from the B & O Railroad. World War II had begun and the canal lay dormant until 1946.

THE FLOOD OF JUNE 24, 1972

The rains of Hurricane Agnes caused considerable damage, cresting at 16.5 feet. Sixty-six miles of towpath were scoured. Major damage included a 300-foot cave-in at the Widewater section of the canal below Great Falls. The Hurricane Agnes flood gained in intensity as it hit Pennsylvania and southern New York. It is remembered as one of the most brutal floods to ever hit those two states. Repairs to the canal and the riverscape took many years to complete, even though sufficient funds had been made available. During the restoration of the canal a great deal of cumulative damage was corrected, including the repair and upgrade of historic flood protection structures to original canal specifications. This was the first serious C & O Canal restoration work since 1889.

THE FLOOD OF NOVEMBER 7, 1985

The Flood of '85, also called "The Killer Flood" by West Virginians, was caused by the rains from Hurricane Juan, more devastating and lethal upriver than the Agnes Flood of June 1972. The intensity,

Flood	Cubic feet per second/per day Chain Bridge, Washington, D.C.
May 30–June 1, 1889	460,000 (est.)
March 24, 1924	295,000
March 19, 1936	484,000*
October 17, 1942	447,000
June 24, 1972	359,000
November 7, 1985	317,000

* Highest velocity ever recorded for the Potomac River equals 275 billion gallons/day. (Average flow is about 7 billion gallons/day.) Lowest recorded flow was in September 1966 at 388 million gallons/day before water supply withdrawals. An average of 400 million gallons of water are withdrawn daily in the Washington area for water supply. Approximately 100 million gallons/day of groundwater is used in rural areas.

damage, and heartache were felt most severely in Virginia and West Virginia where many people died. The American Red Cross estimated that 16,000 homes were destroyed by the flood: 9,313 in West Virginia, 3,500 in Virginia, 2,722 in Pennsylvania, and 412 in Maryland.

In October 1985, a fledgling storm, some 3,500 miles away off the coast of the Sahara Desert in Africa, had just set a course for the United States. By October 31, the storm, now a hurricane and named Juan, made a landfall at Port Arthur, Texas. Spinning out of control, it veered north, carrying deluges of heavy rain as it moved up the Virginia and West Virginia valleys. It then continued into Pennsylvania until it abated on November 6.

On October 31, 1985, the C & O Canal Park went on a flood alert. Something was going on down in the Gulf. A hurricane, recently named Juan, had been trying to chew its way into the mainland, and it looked like a killer. The park staff began making hurried contacts with Leo Harrison, head of the Washington district of the National Weather Service, to size things up. On the weekend of November 2 and 3, relentless torrential rains fell. By Monday, November 4, we knew we had a serious problem on our hands. Water levels were rising at an alarming rate. There was no good news anywhere in the Potomac Basin.

I, as Superintendent of the C & O Canal Park, and my rangers and maintenance employees, had a vested interest in Potomac River floods and near-floods. It is a responsibility never to be taken lightly; when the staff goes on flood alert, a tense note pervades the air. Like it or not, we are suddenly thrust feet first into the center of the action and are held accountable for any drownings within the boundaries of the park. We maintain radio contact throughout the flood as river gauge readings are closely monitored. Readings are continually brought up to date. The chief ranger now becomes the park flood manager above Seneca, and the Palisades manager runs things below Seneca. Together they supervise the actions of the towpath rangers to insure that public safety remains paramount and that everyone in the park receives the identical weather forecasts and water level updates, including the rates of the river rise, and how they are impacting the towpath and park structures.

The park staff at Great Falls was not yet fully aware of the progress of the flood, which was still a full day upriver. Personal contacts were made with people who lived in or around the park to be certain everyone was aware of impending overflows and current river readings. The curious were standing on canal aqueducts, hillsides, and bridges to watch the great event gather momentum. Reluctant citizens were asked to stay away from the fast-moving river. Some would, others would not.

From all reports, this mess was coming from the south. It appeared that the South Branch and the Shenandoah were getting it all. We were into Monday and the rain hadn't let up yet. We were desperate for a fix on what was happening. No one, including the Weather Service, was sure. For some reason the water was not flooding significantly along the North Branch or at Cumberland. The canal below Oldtown was still taking a pounding. The South Branch was sending down loads of ripped trailer pieces all having the flimsy gauge of a beer can. Dead animals, wall-to-wall carpeting, broken window frames, kitchen stoves, washers and dryers, automobiles, propane gas tanks, and pieces of houses, kitchen tables and chairs, and trash piles continued to rush by with more of the same in hot pursuit. Here and

Flood at Dam No. 5, wooden towpath bridge in foreground, November 5, 1985. (Courtesy of the National Park Service)

there knotted strings of Christmas lights caught high in the trees. A giant pile-up at the South Branch confluence was causing the river to run upstream, back towards Cumberland, past Oldtown.

We heard reports on the damage at Springfield, Virginia, in the Moorefield Valley, and along the Shenandoah. Drownings were reported everywhere but there were no details. Still, Cumberland didn't seem to be hit much . . . we didn't understand why. More damage reports came in . . . miles of towpath and underlying banks had been lost. Debris and solid waste continued to pile up on the park for miles. Angry brown water was spilling out over the park as the water continued to rise. Massive tree trunks with huge balls of earth clinging to the roots were crashing into the river banks while others that had broken loose continued to rush downriver. Miles of dead electric wire hung from trees, some of it still carrying pieces of poles and wooden arms.

Rangers moved up and down the towpath, checking and reporting. Radio transmissions began at daylight and continued until late in the night. "Bubba" Swain and others had started to dig out a blowout patch that would eventually wear a huge break in the towpath, allowing rising canal water to rush back into the river. The blowout saved the towpath below Swain's Lock and the lockhouse where the Swain family had lived for several generations.

The National Weather Service projected Little Falls to rise to a river level of 10 feet or more. The Palisades manager passed the word to begin five rows of sandbags around the Great Falls Tavern and down-canal where the towpath elevation was low. My hand-held radio crackled: the floodwaters had crossed the towpath at Pennyfield Lock and were still rising. Below Violettes Lock, paddle-gates were cautiously opened to ease the pressure on the fragile lock gates and to keep as much water out of the canal as possible down in the lower reaches of the canal. Stop planks, placed flat for strength, were inserted in slots on either side of the 28-foot-wide stop gate at the head of Widewater, just above Lock 16. Wide stop planks were hurriedly pulled away from waste weirs (large adjustable openings under the towpath to control overflow water from the canal prism). Wide boards, which sealed off waste weirs, were pulled at several precise locations above Fletchers Boat House to allow excess canal water to pour back into the river.

A report came over the radio: the floodwaters were rushing over the towpath above Fletchers. The blowout patch finally caused a massive cave-in of the towpath below Fletchers. The rushing flow coming down the canal was thankfully diverted back into the river, while chunks of the bank continued to fall toward the river. Floodwaters were now reported to be within 2 inches from the topmost lock stones at Lock No. 3 in Georgetown, where the canal boat was securely tied in the middle of the canal. If the water continued its rise, it would start spilling into the sub-basements of the office and commercial buildings at Lock 3. We were aware that structural damage to the buildings and private homes could reach multimillion dollar proportions.

Finally, the level at Georgetown's Lock 3 held at just 2 inches below the top stones. The blowout patches at Swain's and Fletchers were working! The blowout below Fletchers was near the spot on the towpath where a similar blowout occurred during the Agnes flood, saving houses and office buildings at the Lock 3 level. I was prepared to blow my own patch or have one dug and let the natural erosion do the job. All this had to be done quickly before the water on the towpath rose and gathered strength.

A cresting pattern started upstream and the park cautiously forecasted when the water would begin to recede at locations along the canal. Much of the park had been wrecked. The damage was more severe than originally anticipated. Staffers in Washington and on Capitol Hill were not aware that the flood had hit with such a resounding blow and that the canal waters in Georgetown were approaching dangerous levels. Telephones were jammed with incoming calls for information. Washington office staffers demanded complete repair and restoration estimates for early meetings to be held the following morning. The flood stayed at its highest level for four days. We had been running cumulative estimates since the first day of the rains. They were brought current every day. I had been sleeping fitfully each night in my office chair, awakened periodically by radio reports of new damage and updates on river level projections.

Even before the water receded, pressure continued to mount for a hurried, no-nonsense damage estimate. The moment of truth had arrived. Only the superintendent could handle this one. No one else was authorized to release a total damage estimate. I had to report the figure whether I wanted to or not . . . it would not wait. The staff and I knew full well that once the figure was released, we would be stuck with it. I swallowed hard and made the phone call. My heart was pounding. I told all. Total damage from Cumberland to Georgetown was $9,382,000. Just the trash and solid waste removal and cleanup, before actual repairs could even begin for the 184 1/2-mile canal, would take the first million.

My wife, Sarah, had been trying to contact her mother in Parsons, West Virginia. She couldn't get through. Just after the flood hit the West Virginia panhandle and the Shenandoah area, an awesome silence settled in the valleys. We called the West Virginia State Police Troopers in Elkins and were told that the flood had subsided and "most of Parsons is gone." We refused to believe it!

November 5, 1985—flood damage, Parsons, West Virginia. (Photo by Faith Anne Smith)

We filled the car with food and gallon-jugs of water and zipped over the mountains. We reached Parsons and what we saw was gut-wrenching. Houses along the river were totally wrecked or missing, railroad tracks were twisted and lying in the roadways, people were milling in the streets and in the farm fields, salvaging whatever they could. Everyone seemed to be shoveling deep mounds of mud out of their open windows. Unmatched shoes were lying everywhere, spilled into the streets from the flooded shoe factory at Pulp Mill Bottom.

The A & P Grocery Store was gutted, as were most of the other businesses in town. Soldiers were directing traffic and trying to keep order. There was an ugly parade of trucks and cars from out-of-town spectators circling the streets to get a better look at the destruction and misery with the appearance of vultures enjoying their morbid thrill, tallying up the troubles of others, glad it wasn't them! The town newspaper, *The Parsons Advocate,* had a sharp and direct message for the vultures: "Don't come to Tucker County to gawk!!"

Sarah's mother survived the flood, and the house was intact, but there was a lot of work to be done in Parsons that day and for many more to come.

The West Virginia Governor's Office published a final tally a year after the flood:

Dead	38
Missing	10
Homeless	2,587
Damage estimated	$500 million
Homes destroyed	5,151
Homes, major damage	3,033
Businesses destroyed	154
Businesses, major damage	474
Bridges, closed or need repair	151

Tallies for Virginia, Maryland, and Pennsylvania were proportional.

I stayed in Parsons for three days before I returned to the canal. In my absence, nobody had prepared a budget request. My beautiful park was a 184$\frac{1}{2}$-mile bombed-out, uncovered landfill. Senate Appropriation Committee staffers accepted an invitation to join me on the towpath at the canal side of the Harpers Ferry Bridge to view the carnage. They weren't convinced that the canal should be repaired every time a flood hits, at least not above Great Falls. I thought to myself, given the overall damage figures, "Good grief, gentlemen, I'm only asking for $10 million." But when a request is made for that kind of money, people scatter. They were sympathetic but there was no sign of hope in their voices. My canal constituency might put some pressure on, but this was going to take a long time and if I wasn't careful, I might have a no-win fight on my hands, and nothing would be accomplished. In these kinds of situations, superintendents must act fast. Floods and other natural disasters are soon forgotten, so it is important that repair funds be obtained quickly, immediately after the flood. If not, the money handlers could come back and ask, "What flood?"

The new director of the Park Service and I met at Great Falls. There were no flood repair monies anywhere to be found. I drove back to my office in Sharpsburg with a lead weight in the pit of my stomach. I was going to figure out a way to clean up that mess yet! Before I reached Sharpsburg I had the answer. I would rally my premier constituency—my volunteers: the Boy and Girl Scouts, organized clubs, Canal Association members, canoe clubs, sporting clubs, individuals, and any others who would find it exhilarating to fight the battle by my side. We had nothing to lose. I would promote a C & O Canal Cleanup Camporee. I would shut the park down for the coming year and open it only to clean-up volunteers who loved the canal enough to work for it. The park staff worked all winter, planning and organizing. Rangers were dispatched to Boy Scout meetings held in Maryland and nearby states and signed up volunteers by the troop. Volunteers would receive a volunteer pin, a yellow volunteer hat, and a lifetime supply of plastic trash bags, donated by Hefty Bags, bless 'em. The park furnished all the hand-tools. Volunteers were not allowed to use power tools. By signing the proper forms, the volunteer was covered under Workers' Compensation during the workday, a decided benefit for the public.

The park provided group campsites near the work areas, and furnished potable water and portajohns. The volunteers worked under the supervision of their own scoutmasters or organization leaders, and our park maintenance staff. The Secretary of the Interior was the honored guest at our "kickoff" ceremony on the Potomac Fish and Game Club grounds at Falling Waters, just outside of Williamsport.

Our clean-up program became a centerpiece of Secretary of the Interior Hodel's "Take Pride in America" program, and the park and the volunteers were proud to be a part of it. We received nationwide publicity. Everything from money to bulldozers poured in to help.

We worked hard that year of 1986; the park was cleaned up, slick as a whistle. Approximately 8,700 volunteers had signed up. Aside from some poison ivy and mosquito bites, no one was injured. We saved the taxpayers a cool $1 million in clean-up costs. We hauled solid waste by the tons out of that park. Congresswoman Beverly Byron went out and beat the bushes on the Hill and, in time, Congress became a believer, and released the funds we needed for major repairs. When it was finally over, I was summoned to the White House Rose Garden to represent the park and receive the official kudos that all the volunteers and my staff deserved. The scouts keep coming back every year to follow through on an array of new projects, from growth removal from historic structures to conducting gypsy moth counts from special traps placed along the towpath. This is the ethic Secretary Hodel was striving for. He believed strongly that the youngsters in this nation must be taught that volunteerism is a character-building discipline, and that, in this case, it evoked a personal involvement in the nation's environmental ethic.

With the Bloomington Dam finally in place in time for the November 1985 flood, and poised for a real test, the U.S. Army Corps of Engineers reported that riverside area damage, conservatively estimated at $113 million, was prevented on the North Branch of the Potomac. The dam, with its enormous reserve capacity, held back the floodwaters and spared riverside areas from great volumes of damaging water. Thus, with the reserve capacities of the Bloomington and Savage River dams, and the flood control work set in place in Cumberland in the 1950s, the North Branch received minimal damage from the dam locations to the confluence of the South Branch of the Potomac, some 65 river-miles downstream. The Bloomington Reservoir rose 80 feet in 30 hours at the height of the storm. There was considerable damage above the dam but below the impoundment, people barely got their feet wet.

Without the Bloomington Dam functioning, great damage would have occurred along the North Branch below the reservoir, including irreparable harm at Westvaco Luke paper mill, with nearly 2,000 jobs at stake; the critical waste treatment facility at Westernport; and the many industrial activities along the McMullen Highway (Route 220) below Cumberland.

Chapter 10.

POTOMAC BE DAMMED

The 1780 Laws of the State of Maryland ceded to the Congress of the United States part of a 10-square-mile district, including part of the Potomac River and its bed, to be used for the seat of government. A similar action was undertaken by the Commonwealth of Virginia. Agreements were signed in Suter's Tavern in Georgetown, Maryland, and the land was subsequently accepted by the Congress. On March 30, 1791, President George Washington proclaimed that the area had been selected as the location of the nation's capital. Suter's Tavern has often been referred to as the "Birthplace of the District of Columbia."

In 1846, the portion of the 10 square miles lying south of the Potomac River that had been ceded to the Congress by the Commonwealth of Virginia was ceded back to Virginia without so much as a constitutional amendment. It was determined that Congress would not require the Virginia parcel for the nation's capital.

In 1853, a Presidential Order directed that water be brought to Washington City. Quality and quantity would henceforth be the responsibility of the U.S. Army Corps of Engineers. Up to this time, residents of Alexandria, Virginia, and Georgetown, Maryland, were obtaining their water from numerous springs and wells. An ample supply of good quality ground water was readily available for limited domestic use. At the time of the establishment of Washington City, in 1792, the only reference to a city water supply was made by architect Pierre Charles L'Enfant who noted, "Piney Creek [now Rock Creek] whose water, if necessary, may supply the city . . . "

The first municipal water system in Washington City consisted of water piped from the old City Spring in 1802. Wooden pipes made of bored logs joined together with short wrought-iron pipe connections were used to convey the water from the spring to a few houses on Pennsylvania Avenue and to Woodward's Tavern. By 1865, 1,382 wells were in service. The municipal pump repairman was the busiest man in town. Water from these wells was highly potable and some waters were said to possess medicinal qualities and were prized. The first house to have running water was the old Van Ness mansion located on the site of the present Pan American building. The pipes were installed in 1820 connecting the mansion to the wells on the grounds.

After the 1853 Presidential Order calling for water in the capital city, the Potomac River, especially in the vicinity of the District of Columbia, was bristling with an array of laws and federal regulations designed to manage and monitor water quantity and quality. The Congress, through a succession of District of Columbia and military committees and subcommittees was charged with overseeing the District's water supply. It was quickly realized that a reliable water supply for the nation's capital would require broad Potomac River Basin planning, management, and monitoring. What happened along the river and its shores at Piedmont and Westernport, Maryland, some 220 miles upstream, had its effects at the end of the pipe, in Washington. Water not only had to be supplied to Washington, D.C., but reliable quantities were also needed for the communities upriver. Vast quantities of water were required for agriculture, industry, residential use, and to maintain a ready conduit for burgeoning sewage and siltation loads that were becoming a way of life. Was this the river of George Washington, furnishing an abundance of fish for everyone to eat, where the earliest plantations were established by its settlers, where Indian tribes flourished, where names of tributaries, large and small, echo with familiarity for American ears—Bull Run, the Shenandoah, the Monocacy, St. Mary's, and Antietam Creek?

One hundred years ago, those who used the river sensed that the reckless logging practices of the late nineteenth century throughout the upper basin were changing the character of the river. At that time, river runners and farmers noted a continuing increase in silt in the river and accelerating runoffs. The long-term effects of irresponsible logging were discussed and written about, but little was done about it. The long-term effects of soil erosion were simply not understood, and there were no reliable techniques to measure losses or to interpret such findings.

The closing days of the nineteenth century were days of progress and wealth. Senator Chauncey Depew of New York aptly summed up the times when he asserted, "There isn't a man here that does not feel 400 percent bigger than he did in 1896 . . . bigger intellectually, and bigger patriotically." No longer was this an agrarian nation, but a nation obsessed with progress at any price and wealth by any means. Our natural resources were believed to be there for the taking and, even today, this attitude is prevalent. In the late 1890s, the outlook that there was no tomorrow to worry about seemed to be the accepted doctrine.

Almost fifty years later, problems of increased population were fully felt in the Potomac River Basin. In the 1940s, the condition of the Potomac River had hit bottom. It was laughed at, noses were pinched at its foul odors, and citizens were warned not to swim in the river or eat the fish. Solutions were always predictable, centering around the building of massive dams. "Dams," it was said, "are needed on every tributary until there are no tributaries left."

In the opinion of the U.S. Army Corps of Engineers, the only way to insure an adequate water supply was to hold water back by storing it, causing draw-down problems and visual blight. All this conjecture was advanced in the computer stone age. Accordingly, sophisticated and enlightened modeling of water sources and volumes was not available. In addition, today's cry, "Clean it up before you put it in the river" meant little in view of the paucity of funds to put waste treatment facilities on line in critical areas. The likelihood of towns and communities along the river cleaning up their waste water in treatment plants was remote indeed. After all, waste was always dumped in the Potomac River, and it then became the next downriver town's problem. At the end of the chain, the final town was Washington, D.C., where the load slogged back and forth in a tidewater broth at the Capital's door. The stinking stew included raw sewage, beds of dead fish, burgeoning siltation, toxic industrial wastes, and the rest of the turbid flotsam of man's callous and feckless river legacy. Plans were piecemeal at best, and all required lots of money. The only money ever available was for planning and more planning.

In 1956 the Congress directed the U.S. Army Corps of Engineers to undertake a basinwide study to develop plans for flood control and the conservation of land and water resources. Congress was looking for a long-term solution to the basin's water supply problems. Seven years later, the Corps published its nine-volume *Potomac River Basin Report*. The report was monumental in size and scope, and recommended as a solution the construction of no less than 16 major, multipurpose basin reservoirs on the Potomac and its tributaries, which would reverse the public's longstanding philosophy of free-flowing stream systems and inundate 35 miles of the C & O Canal to create a reservoir stretching up the Monocacy River to near Frederick, Maryland, and up the Shenandoah River on its way to Front Royal, Virginia. Thousands upon thousands of acres of productive valley lands would be acquired, then inundated, with all inhabitants relocated. The proposals were received with loud and vehement rejection at local, state, and congressional levels, causing a shrill public outcry that still echoes through the valley today.

I was a part of that vocal groundswell, and attended meeting after meeting up and down the valley as a part of the seemingly impotent opposition to this grand and destructive design. I fully expected it to happen. A great deal of the focus was on the key Seneca Dam, to be built on the Potomac mainstem just above Washington. At the time, the U.S. Army Corps of Engineers, certainly a proud and vastly capable agency, lost a lot of its credibility, at least in the Washington area and the Potomac Basin environs, as a consequence of their recommendations as presented in the *Potomac River Basin Report*.

The Corps to this day remains defensive over the continued public harping about a report published almost thirty years ago. They are quick to remind those Potomac riverphiles who refuse to forget that it is Congress that passes the laws and makes the final decisions in these matters. One weak link in that argument is the fact that Congress usually acts on the supported recommendations of the agency advancing the plans and recommendations. After having mellowed these past thirty years, I don't think it was the final nine-volume recommendations that surprised river and canal watchers, for we were always expecting the worst. Instead, it was the blatant insensitivities underlying the proposals that aroused public outcry. After all, wasn't this the nation's capital? The River Bend Proposal would have inundated over 35 miles of canal, including historic structures, locks, and lockhouses. The public, especially those who have deep roots in this long-settled region, cherish the scenic and historic treasures of the valley that, in turn, bring about a sense of well-being and place to its citizens. Furthermore, the needs of tourism, not just Capital tourists, but visitors to the rolling piedmont, Civil War battlefields, and the beautiful river vistas, would also be severely impacted.

The conservationists saw a large worm crawling across a delicate rose, and it stirred the juices of retaliation and do or die resistance. Bird watchers became Corps watchers; legal action was planned and, with the release of the Corps' report, conservation groups, especially those along the river and the canal, began to grow in membership. A coordinating committee on the Potomac River Valley was formed to oppose the dams and the effective Citizens' Committee on Natural Resources, which had been opposing the Corps' plans for years, was still actively fighting. The committee circulated their excellent report, *Potomac Prospect,* and Tony Smith, who was destined to pull the C & O Canal Park chestnut out of the fire at a later date, assembled a strong coalition of conservation organizations, citizens' action groups, and businessmen that, collectively, articulately opposed the Corps' report to the Congress.

In his State of the Union Message of 1965, President Lyndon Johnson declared that the time had come "to identify and preserve free-flowing stretches of our great scenic rivers before growth and development make the beauty of the unspoiled waterway a memory." President Johnson turned the Corps proposal over to Interior Secretary Stewart Udall, with instructions to prepare a conservation plan for the Potomac River with the ultimate goal of assuring an adequate supply of water for decades, and providing flood protection. Further, Secretary Udall was instructed to protect the beauty of the river and its basin, and to plan for full recreational opportunities. President Johnson's charge seized the imagination of a public grown weary of the continuing threats to the river, and at the same time focused attention on the more unacceptable aspects of the Corps' report. With this turn of events there was no further role for the Corps. The nine-volume *Potomac River Basin Report* now languishes on the shelf, the sole reminder of intense planning and the search for answers along the Potomac that spanned a 40-year period.

Any discussion of dams or flood protection structures on the Potomac River or its tributaries must include the story of the Bloomington Dam (Jennings Randolph Reservoir), authorized by the Flood Control Act of 1962. Construction began in 1971 and took ten years to complete. The project straddles the North Branch of the Potomac River between Garrett County, Maryland, and Mineral County, West Virginia, 8 miles above Bloomington, Maryland.

The Bloomington project goes back at least 30 years, to a 1961 report by the U.S. Army Corps of Engineers that examined the water resources of the North Branch of the Potomac. The Corps has recommended many other reservoirs for the Potomac Basin since 1961, but the Bloomington project is the only Corps project that has survived the unyielding onslaughts of public debate over the years. In proposing the original project, the U.S. Army Corps of Engineers picked a site near Bloomington, choosing the town's name for the project. Subsequently, it was discovered that the site was honeycombed with abandoned coal mines, and was unusable. The project was moved 8 miles upstream but kept the old name: the Bloomington Dam and Lake. To put things right, the project was rededicated in May 1987, after West Virginia Senator Jennings Randolph, who was instrumental in making this and other water resource projects across the nation a reality.

The location of the Bloomington Dam (Jennings Randolph Reservoir) is unique and produces a better and bigger bang for the $175 million it cost to construct than most Corps reservoirs. The North Branch of the Potomac has historically suffered from severe water pollution from acid mine drainage. The successful marketing of coal in the Georges Creek area began when the Baltimore and Ohio Railroad reached Cumberland in 1842, with the Chesapeake and Ohio Canal right on its heels in 1850. Thus, with transportation outlets now firmly established, the mining frenzy began in earnest and there was no tomorrow. The portion of the rich coal seam known as the "Big Vein" in the Georges Creek field was only a part of a huge coal vein that stretched over 900 miles from Pennsylvania to Alabama. In addition, quality, low-ash, low-sulphur coal was being discovered up and down the ridges below Cumberland, creating yet more mines that were later abandoned. When this occurred, many owners ducked, leaving the land riddled with mine holes and gob piles. The mines also exposed deposits of sulfites, aluminum, and other minerals that caused serious environmental problems when deposited into nearby streams. These substances turn the water acidic, leaching aluminum and other metals into the water. The acidity and metals permit only the hardiest forms of life to survive.

In addition to all this, the North Branch flows through narrow, steep valleys, causing periodic deluges of floodwaters. The two major North Branch problems are today being mitigated; less acidity is being released downstream of the Bloomington Dam. What makes the difference in downstream water quality today is the selective process used to release water. Inside a 330-foot-high control tower, surrounded by water up to its 250-foot mark, water in the reservoir can be sampled at various depths. When acid hits the big lake it tends to stratify and separate, like oil and vinegar salad dressing in the refrigerator. A determination is then made as to how much acid there is and where it is. By opening pairs of gates, each pair located at a different depth in the lake, the best available mixtures of water and acid can be diverted downstream. At summer pool the lake stores about 31 billion gallons of water that can be used for water supply downstream. A minimum flow of 93 cubic feet per second or about 60 million gallons of water per day is maintained in the river downstream of the dam. Releases are coordinated with those from the nearby

Jennings Randolph Reservoir is 250 feet deep. The intake tower is 330 feet high with six intake levels. (Courtesy of the Interstate Commission on the Potomac River Basin)

Savage River Dam to maintain the best possible water quality for the North Branch.

As a result of the downpour during the infamous 1985 flood, the Bloomington Lake Reservoir rose 80 feet in 30 hours and came to within 6 feet of the top of the dam's gates. Without the dam, the total estimated damage from the 1985 flood on the North Branch below the dam could have been $113 million. By holding back the floodwaters, the dam spared riverside areas from destructive volumes of water, and slowed down the river's velocity. Charles Walker,

spokesman for the U.S. Army Corps of Engineers, reported in the local papers that the stretch of land between Hancock and the Monocacy River at Frederick, Maryland, would have sustained $1.1 mil-
lion more in damage had the dam not been built. At Paw Paw, West
Virginia, the flood would have climbed 2½ feet higher than the 54-
foot river level that flooded the entire downtown, causing $11 mil-
lion in damages. "This [the height of the flood waters] doesn't sound
like much," Walker said, "but it sure means a lot when you spread it
over the land."

The Bloomington Dam project cost $175 million, and the damage
prevented in the November 1985 event alone was estimated at $113
million, a most favorable cost-benefit ratio, hard to match anywhere.
In addition, the Savage River Dam and several small flood control
projects in Allegany and Garrett counties prevented an estimated $54
million in damages. By comparison, when in flood, the uncontrolled
South Branch of the Potomac ripped out entire towns in West Virginia, causing $200 million in damage and dozens of deaths.

When the Corps initially proposed sixteen dams in the Potomac
Basin in their 1963 *Potomac River Basin Report,* I was skeptical of
the Bloomington project. Most of the imagined horrors the Corps
served up in those days never came about, and the water supply
problems in Washington, D.C., were finally resolved by skilled
"modeling" (carefully working out a plan) to better program the
flows of existing water sources and computer-testing various ideas.
The Corps had been working on plans to insure water supply for the
nation's capital since 1924, and only the tried and true techniques to
cut down pollution and store water were valid. Corps engineers still
say, tongue in cheek, "The only solution to pollution is dilution."

In 1975, I accompanied Gilbert Gude on portions of his now famous fact-finding hike down the Potomac River. The Bloomington
Dam was one of our first stops along the upper North Branch. We
walked the floor of the dam where the workmen were filling and
grouting, and I must confess, I couldn't figure out what it was all
about at the time. The word "massive" was the word most frequently used in my notes, massive in size, massive in its vast storage volume, massive in terms of its silent mission. My opinion was that this
dam was needed, and it has subsequently proved that it works. Some

42 percent of the dam's function deals with improved water quality, 33 percent with increased water supply downstream of the dam, 22 percent to reduce flood damage, and the balance dedicated to public recreation. The Bloomington Dam controls a drainage area of 263 square miles, or 20 percent of the North Branch sub-basin. I had to see it before I was willing to believe it.

Chapter 11.

GUARDIANS OF THE RIVER

To follow the progress of the healing of the Potomac River from 1940 to the present, there is no better bellwether than to review the chronological highlights of the last fifty years, recently released by the Interstate Commission on the Potomac River Basin (ICPRB). The Interstate Commission was established under interstate compact and by an act of Congress in 1940. Members of the commission are the signatories to the compact (Maryland, Virginia, West Virginia, Pennsylvania, and the District of Columbia) and the federal government. The commission and its successive staffs have been totally immersed in the healing of the Potomac River virtually on a day-by-day basis since July 1940 when the U.S. Congress gave its consent to create the Potomac Valley Conservation District and established the Interstate Commission on the Potomac River Basin.

In its recent commemorative publication, *Healing a River, the Potomac: 1940–1990,* the Interstate Commission outlined decade by decade the extraordinary progress made in cleaning up the Potomac River since the establishment of the commission in 1940 to the end of 1990. This is the story of one of the most dramatic environmental reversals of this century, made even more significant by the additional responsibility of the region to sustain impeccable water quality standards and sufficient quantities of potable water to serve a burgeoning population. In 1940, the Potomac River was one grand environmental mess, and destined to get worse long before it got better.

The chronology in the ICPRB report is paraphrased below and sets out the major contributions to a clean water commitment made by the Interstate Commission, federal, state, and local agencies, and many others since 1940. The chronology was prepared by the Interstate Commission's Associate Director of Public Affairs, Beverly Bandler. It is a professional review of the hard work and unceasing commitment by those who have served the public well during these past fifty years. Without this continuing massive effort, it is anyone's guess as to what the Potomac River's water quality and quantity indices would reveal today. The story is also one of a constantly changing technology that, in 1940, could only be called primitive and unreliable. All this was changed by advanced techniques in monitoring, modeling, ever-expanding computer capabilities, and a new and aggressive breed of water quality engineers and scientists.

HEALING A RIVER 1940–1990: FIFTY YEARS IN THE LIFE OF THE POTOMAC

In 1940, the basin's population was 1.7 million, approximately half of which were living in or near the vicinity of Washington, D.C. In the first comprehensive survey of the Potomac Basin's water resources, the Interstate Commission stated in 1943 that only 9 percent of that population was served by complete (secondary) sewage treatment plants, and 80 percent by only primary treatment plants. About 11 percent of the basin's population had no sewage treatment facilities whatsoever.

Serious water quality problems were apparent in all the basin's fifteen major cities and towns, but the three main trouble spots were in the Luke-Cumberland, Maryland, area; along the Shenandoah River where development had recently begun; and in Washington, D.C. Most of the basin's residents were dependent on the Potomac and its tributaries for their daily water supply. The commission's mid-decade findings revealed that 184 water supplies were taken from surface streams, of which 131 of these were public water systems, and the balance served industries.

In those days, the Blue Plains Waste Water Treatment Plant within the District of Columbia was only a primary treatment plant, designed basically to settle solids from 130 million gallons per day of combined storm and sanitary sewer waters before discharging them into the Potomac River. Blue Plains' capacity had been planned for only 650,000 citizens, and was believed to be adequate until 1950, but in reality the plant was overloaded soon after it began operating in 1938. By 1943, the population in the Metropolitan Washington Area (MWA) had increased to a point where Blue Plains had to be expanded, yet its capacity was still running behind loadings, and the resulting sludge from the Blue Plains plant was becoming a problem in itself.

In the upper basin, an estimated 173,000 pounds of acid from abandoned coal mines were added daily to sewage burdens. Many North Branch Potomac streams were left barren and devoid of aquatic life. In addition, considerable siltation resulting from poor farming practices above Washington particularly in the Monocacy and Goose Creek watersheds, were readily apparent. Silt-producing tobacco farming was still the principal crop in the lower Potomac. By 1949, the annual "mud load" dumped into the Potomac would be estimated at well over 1.7 million tons.

Since the 1920s, the Potomac at Washington had experienced a series of nuisance plant infestations, dominated by the water chestnut. In the 1940s, it was replaced with Eurasian water milfoil and a small incidence of blue-green algae. Complaints about mosquito-filled mudflats and swamps below the District increased; attempts were made to cover the flats with oil, or simply fill them in.

In the 1940s almost all areas of the Potomac Valley depended to some extent on water for recreation, especially fishing. Commercial fishing was also carried out in the lower portion of the tidal Potomac and its tributaries, but was steadily declining. The decline was compounded by political conflict between Maryland and Virginia over fishing rights.

The Interstate Commission and the states worked to help solve the

Potomac's many problems. A range of professionals participated in the commission's first step to identify and map the basin's conditions, and collect data, particularly from industries. The next step was the commission's proposed water-quality criteria and "standards map," adopted by the states in 1946. The following year, the commission adopted a cooperative water-quality sampling program. The commission reviewed pollution legislation throughout the basin states and the District of Columbia, and encouraged improved laws. The states listened. Most importantly, in that decade, the commission supported federal financial assistance for sewage treatment plant construction, emphasizing state enforcement.

The Potomac paid heavily in the 1950s for post-war growth. As the decade opened, the chairman of the Interstate Commission put it bluntly, "The water of the Potomac River throughout its length is unsuitable for drinking without treatment. At and above Great Falls, the river is unquestionably unsuitable for drinking without treatment and questionably safe for swimming. From Hains Point to Key Bridge, the river is questionably safe for recreation. The Anacostia River below Bladensburg and the Potomac River from Hains Point to Fort Foote are unsuitable for any purpose." The Potomac was believed to be second only to the port of Houston, Texas, as a pollution delivery system. The upper and middle portions of the river and several spots along the Potomac's main tributaries such as the Shenandoah, however, were forced to cope with wastes well beyond their assimilative capacity. In 1950, there were 87 sewage treatment plants in the basin, with only about half considered adequate.

The river in the upper basin was receiving mostly untreated waste discharges from over 100 industrial plants, in addition to municipal waste. Here the river was also subject to acid mine drainage. The 6-mile segment that flowed within the Metropolitan Washington Area from Hains Point to Fort Foote was referred to as an "open sewer." It received the sewage from the District of Columbia, Montgomery and Prince Georges counties, Maryland, and Arlington and Fairfax counties, and the city of Alexandria, Virginia. In that portion of the Potomac, algal blooms and fish kills dominated the summer months and would do so until 1977. In the late 1950s, observed dissolved oxygen levels were sometimes less than one part per million in the area between Giesboro Point (on the south shore of the Anacostia River) and Fort Foote.

The commission determined that the metropolitan river could assimilate a pollution load equivalent to 475,000 people, but by 1950, the area population was 1.5 million, and the Blue Plains plant could remove only 20 percent of the pollution. Other issues loomed as well. There were not enough sites for thousands of tons of sludge generated by the improved sewage treatment plant. In addition, it was calculated that if the upper basin erosion rate were to continue unchecked, the Potomac River from Chain Bridge to Fort Foote would be filled in 50 years. The water demand was multiplying, and had become a serious concern by mid-decade. As a result of a basinwide water resources study, initiated by the U.S. Army Corps of Engineers, it was determined that the river was being used as a dumping ground; recreation facilities were inadequate; there was a lack of trained water pollution control personnel, as well as inadequate financing for the overtaxed sewer system. In the face of all these problems, there was a recognized lack of coordination among the dozens of agencies concerned with basin water resources. As if the river did not have enough problems, shoot-outs had occurred between Maryland's oyster police and watermen who were harvesting the river's riches by illegal dredging, which continued into the 1950s.

Larger basin municipalities and the metropolitan Virginia counties committed themselves to the expansion of their waste treatment facilities. A study of the metro area's sewage determined that the perspective was now regional, and interjurisdictional agreements accomplished by the end of the decade would set the course for the eventual clean-up of the metropolitan Washington river from "point sources." Public support for treatment plant construction on the Potomac was one of the commission's major themes at the close of the decade, and matters began to improve dramatically.

In the upper basin, clean-up efforts had paid off by early 1962, when it was reported that "there are now only 18 raw sewage sources above Washington's water supply intakes . . . with a total population of no more than 25,000." By this date, only one major industry did not provide for waste treatment, but had construction underway. The acid mine drainage in that area increased, however, as mining activities escalated. In one creek alone, the acid load increased more than 100 percent from 1968 to 1973, almost entirely due to strip mining.

The focal point during this decade was the Metropolitan Washington Area, where, by 1960, there were more than 2 million people who would produce a "roaring suburban tide" that would drain the central city and pave 500,000 acres of farmland with houses. Stately monuments of the nation's capital looked out on a "national disgrace," a river that was a tangle of logs, trash, and frequent raw sewage. During the summer and early fall, mats of blue-green algae extended for some 50 miles below the city, blocking sunlight and reducing life-giving oxygen supplies to the water. The sight of thousands of dead fish belly-up and rotting in the river was troubling but common.

Eating fish caught along Washington's shores was prohibited, and so was swimming. The commission's monitoring of water quality showed that in 1965 coliform bacteria levels in the area were 500 times greater than the permissible body-contact limit for swimmable waters. All the while, the demand for water-related recreation was growing.

Water supply problems became acute in 1966, when a 5-year drought reduced the river's daily flow to an all-time low of 388 million gallons, nearly matching the year's highest daily water intake. Sediment from the agricultural upper basin and the suburban mid-basin continued to pour into the river. Sediment studies would accelerate throughout the 1960s, with increasing attention given to urban as well as agricultural areas. The results of the U.S. Geological Survey's (USGS) basinwide study requested by ICPRB in 1960 revealed that the average sediment load to the Potomac River was about 2.5 million tons, most of it discharged during a few storm events each year, and that areas undergoing increased urban growth in the Metropolitan Washington Area had the highest sediment yields.

Comprehensive river basin planning was the buzzword of the 1960s and most important, was the thrust of the federal government into water resources management. This thrust would significantly benefit the Potomac. In 1961, President John F. Kennedy urged the establishment of river basin commissions (a proposal that would lead to the Water Resources Research Act of 1965). Also, in 1961, amendments to the Federal Water Pollution Control Act increasing enforcement authority and funds for waste water treatment plant construction and research signaled a more solidified congressional interest in water quality. In 1963, the comprehensive Potomac Basin plan recommended by the U.S. Army Corps of Engineers would spark years of water supply controversy, to which President Lyndon B. Johnson responded by appointing an interagency task force.

In his 1965 State of the Union address to Congress, Johnson pledged to clean up the nation's rivers, and urged that the Potomac become a "model of beauty and recreation for the entire country." His administration was committed to using "new conservation concepts . . . and patterns of cooperation." In this climate, the Water Quality Act was passed in 1965, establishing a Federal Water Pollution Control Agency and requiring water quality standards.

The condition of the Potomac River in the Metropolitan Washington Area could not respond quickly to the spate of federal legislation and institutional changes, the fervor of waste water treatment plant construction efforts, the improved technology that brought new efficiencies and advanced treatment, a public newly aroused and incensed by the condition of the Potomac, and a new sense by many that it was the "Nation's River." By 1969, the clean-up goals for the Potomac seemed more elusive than ever and the Potomac Enforcement Conference was recalled, fulfilling the 1966 request of the Interstate Commission on the Potomac River Basin. The condition of the river was summarized at that conference: "The Potomac is a severe threat to the health of anyone coming in contact with it . . . . It is grossly polluted."

An increasingly committed public began to see the light, sensitized by Rachel Carson's book, *Silent Spring*. The commission was asked by the Potomac Enforcement Conference to play an active role in carrying out the 1969 recommendations, and with broadened investigatory and coordination authority, approved by its signatories, was prepared to do so.

For a decade that was to have a happy ending, the 1970s did not begin auspiciously. Acid mine drainage had increased in the upper basin as the result of a mining revival, but the magnitude of the problems in the Metropolitan Washington Area made it the main focus of attention. Local treatment plants were overloaded, poorly construct-ed sewer lines were leaking, a sewer pipe gap along the Georgetown waterfront discharged between 15 and 25 million gallons of raw sewage a day until 1972. One-fifth of the mud in the Potomac River now came from the developing area around the nation's capital, and almost no submerged aquatic plants were present in the river. In 1972, fear of cholera and other aerosol-borne diseases contributed to the shutdown of the floating fountain at the end of East Potomac Park, donated as part of Lady Bird Johnson's beautification efforts. In the late 1970s, levels of arsenic and mercury heightened the con-cern about toxins. In 1972, Hurricane Agnes added a brutal blow, flooding the lower river with fresh water to within 12 miles of its mouth, and accelerating the already serious decline in the Potomac's oyster production.

A hopeful sign was evident by mid-decade, algal mats in the upper Potomac estuary were occurring later in the summer and were thin-ner by 1973. Nevertheless, it was concluded in 1975 that, of 23 key Potomac River Basin segments, only 5 had improved and 18 had re-mained the same or had deteriorated since 1962. The trends made reaching the 1983 goal of "swimmable, fishable" waters unlikely.

These bad times for the river were further complicated by con-straints not anticipated at the 1969 conference: plans to incinerate sludge, accumulating at the rate of nearly 1,300 tons a day by the end of the decade, was not a viable option. The 1970 energy crisis and inflation made earlier pollution control cost projections obsolete.

On the water supply scene, it was projected in 1975 that the Met-ropolitan Washington Area would see shortages by 1980, and no so-lution was in sight. A massive pump failure in addition to a drought in 1977 left almost 2 million people in Virginia and Maryland with a fear of dry faucets. The lack of visible signs of improvement in the river in the face of ongoing treatment plant construction, the threat of a lack of a dependable source of water, and nature's own threats caused concern in the public sector throughout the decade of the 1970s.

In spite of the 1970 memorandum of agreement, signed by local governments and intended for the purpose of meeting the lofty 1969 goals, there was actually little agreement for the better part of the decade. Disagreement was rife, particularly over nutrient control strategies, among local and state water quality managers and federal enforcement officials. Each group seemed to blame the others for river conditions. Most of the decade was marked by proposals, counterproposals, lawsuits, and meetings that left significant matters unresolved, and attitudes bitter. Regional efforts fared better in the outer basin than in the Metropolitan Washington Area, where local autonomy was fiercely guarded until the end of the decade.

The heat of the struggle cooled in the last several years of the 1970s. Spurred on by a committed public, the media spotlight, strengthened institution arrangements, new legislative initiatives (especially sediment and storm water control laws and regulations), and technological improvements along with innovative applications, government agencies began to find solutions based upon cooperation. The Low Flow Allocation Agreement (1978), and the formation of the commission's section for Cooperative Water Supply Operations on the Potomac (COOP) (1979), financed by the three major metro Washington area water utilities, reflected new attitudes and approaches.

By the end of the 1970s the Metropolitan Washington Area boasted not only of cooperation between various groups and agencies, but the completion of ambitious treatment plant improvements, rediscovery of the Potomac by pleasure boaters, a rise in the prevalence of large-mouth bass, annual raft races, fishing tournaments, and even full-time fishing guides. There were statistical signs of progress in 1979 as well: decreases in phosphorus and organic carbon (by at least 50 percent), nitrogen and biochemical oxygen demand (37 percent), and chlorophyll (29 percent), and an increase in dissolved oxygen (10 percent).

An ambitious effort to provide sufficient waste water treatment throughout the basin was largely achieved by 1980. Concerns began to shift from "point" (pipe associated) to "nonpoint" (diffuse) pollution sources. A commission study of basin status and trends over the 1973-1984 period revealed good signs. Bacteria, temperature, and turbidity levels were generally down, and dissolved oxygen was up at some stations. Acidity remained high in the Potomac's headwaters, and nutrient levels had increased in agricultural areas, however. By 1986, as a result of improved and expanded treatment, pollution discharges from waste water facilities had declined by more than 90 percent since 1970.

Other signs of improvement included fish (even trout) being caught in the North Branch of the Potomac. There were increasing numbers and diversity of fish, as well as submerged aquatic vegetation in the upper Potomac estuary and the Anacostia River. Improved water quality also brought a resurgence of interest in rejuvenating deteriorated urban waterfronts. An estimated 100,000 people celebrated a cleaner, fishable, Potomac River at a special program called "The Awakening" on the Mall, and a decade of waterfront festivals began in 1981.

Water quality successes were paralleled by a solution to the Metropolitan Washington Area water supply story: multijurisdictional agreements on the operation of the newly constructed Bloomington and Little Seneca dams ended drought fears. The basin received worldwide recognition when the international canoe and kayak competitions were held in 1988 and 1989 on the Savage River.

Remaining problems included acid mine drainage, nutrient removal, sludge disposal, sediment, chlorine, and the decline of fish populations in some fisheries. The six-year EPA study of the Chesapeake Bay, of which the Potomac is an integral part, found that submerged aquatic vegetation, oyster spat set, and freshwater-spawning finfish landings had declined, while nutrients, depleted oxygen zones, and levels of heavy metals and toxins had increased. The 1983 and 1987 Chesapeake Bay Agreements helped to accelerate the Potomac commitment to resolve these issues. Phosphate detergent bans, recommended by the Council of Governments in 1981 and reinforced by the 1983 Chesapeake Bay study, were implemented by Maryland in 1985, then by the District, Virginia, and Pennsylvania.

During this period, the basin states followed up their Chesapeake Bay clean-up commitment on sediment by accelerating enforcement at the local levels, and by effecting stronger storm-water control and encouraging best management practices. The U.S. Army Corps of Engineers made attempts to control hydrilla, the exotic aquatic plant, and also the serious shoreline erosion along the lower Potomac.

Continuing declines in some fish species including shad, striped bass, yellow perch, and large and small-mouth bass, resulted in restrictions, including bans on shad in 1980 and on striped bass in 1985, on both recreational and commercial harvesting to reduce fishing pressure. Bans made anglers unhappy. They were pleased, however, when in 1988, Blue Plains added a process for removing residual chlorine, toxic to juvenile fish, from plant effluent before discharge. Toxins, historically less of a concern due to the lack of industry in the basin, got increasing attention because of upper basin well water and fish contamination, as other pollution problems abated. Efforts were initiated to address these concerns.

Multijurisdictional and multiagency cooperation was reflected in the 1984 Sludge Disposal Agreement, the 1984 and 1987 Anacostia Watershed Restoration Agreements, the 1985 Metro Potomac Safety Pact, and the 1987 West Virginia/Maryland Abandoned Mine Drainage Study. For the past fifty years, the Interstate Commission on the Potomac River Basin, along with numerous other agencies, groups, and individuals, has worked to improve the value of the river for everyone. The road to healing the Potomac's ills has been a long one, and a tribute to continuing cooperation among all those who have participated.

Chapter 12.
CHASING RAINBOWS

The future looks bright and we hope it will not take another fifty years to deal with the remaining environmental problems of the Potomac River. Acid mine drainage, while it can never be totally eliminated in our lifetimes, can be controlled on the North Branch through selective releases from the Jennings Randolph Reservoir. The quality of the water presently being released can average out at a pH of from 5 to $6\frac{1}{2}$. Believe it or not, flows being released at the Jennings Randolph Reservoir tail race today are sustaining a trout fishery from the spillway, 8 miles down the North Branch, to the Westvaco paper plant at Luke, Maryland.

The waste treatment facility at Westernport (the Upper Potomac River Commission) serves not only the surrounding communities, but treats large waste loads from the Luke paper mill. The state, in October 1990, issued a revised and stricter discharge permit to the Westvaco paper plant calling for more complex studies and testing of present discharge qualities. Westvaco, as usual, is willing to participate in this new venture, as the results of the more complex tests that go with the new permit will, once and for all, shed new light on the issue of dioxins on the North Branch. Dioxins are suspected of causing cancer. Warnings were issued in June 1990 after unacceptable levels of dioxin were detected in fish samples taken from the immediate area downstream from the Westvaco paper mill at Luke, Maryland. In March 1992, *The Daily Mail,* in Hagerstown, Maryland, announced that the Maryland Department of the Environment, after almost a year of sampling, had determined that dioxin levels in fish tissue had decreased and that it was safe for the public to eat unlimited amounts of sport fish or "top feeders," like bass, trout, and walleye. The public was advised to still avoid eating "bottom feeders," like channel catfish and bullhead varieties; tests on sunfish were incomplete. Since July 1988, Westvaco has reduced dioxin in its wastewater by more than 90 percent, according to a statement issued by Maryland Secretary of the Environment, Robert Perciasepe.

Testing at the Upper Potomac River Commission in Westernport is under the direction of George H. Shoemaker, plant superintendent. George Shoemaker treats some 115 tons of waste every day, most of it generated from the paper plant. It is interesting to note that in the froth below the treatment plant, below the Westvaco mill, George recently caught an astonishing nine different species of fish.

Fish species in the 8-mile fishery from the dam spillway to Luke include the native Maryland brook trout (a world-class game fish, *Salmo trutta*), "one of the most gorgeous fish that swims anywhere," according to Bob Bachman, chief of Fresh Water Fisheries with Maryland's Department of Natural Resources. In addition, in that 8 miles above Luke, rainbow trout, from introduced fingerlings, are thriving along with brown trout. These trout are in the 4 to 6 pound range.

Large-mouth bass are now plentiful below Washington. In 1989, President George Bush and Justice Sandra Day O'Connor each caught large-mouth bass on the Potomac River in the Metropolitan Washington Area, not far from the White House. In addition to large-mouth bass, there are now 77 species of fish in the Potomac tidewater. Surveys of rockfish reproduction in the Potomac River reveal that spawns are more successful than in any other bay tributary. Certainly, better water quality and the return of grasses are important factors.

National Audubon avian winter counts below Washington continue to show a dramatic increase in the numbers of waterfowl. Increas-

Justice Sandra Day O'Connor catching a large-mouth bass in the Potomac at Washington. (Photo by Susan Noonan, Maryland Public Television, Outdoors Maryland)

ing numbers of eagles and great blue herons at Mason Neck, below Mount Vernon, are important indicators of a more stable and healthy river environment.

The continuing problem of nitrogen and phosphorus is particularly damaging to the river, but the basin states of Maryland and Virginia are presently conducting programs to correct farm practices, and anticipate that these programs will be well along by the mid-1990s.

The first comprehensive survey of tidal Potomac River submerged aquatic vegetation (SAV) began in 1978, under the U.S. Geological Survey, in cooperation with the U.S. Fish and Wildlife Service. The four-year survey documented the present distribution and abundance of SAV and demonstrated a significant change from the early 1930s. Between 1961 and 1978 most of the 15 species of SAV were located in the transition zone between the upper tidal freshwater Potomac

Egret along the Potomac at Mason Neck. (Photo by Nicholas Dean)

and the estuary. In 1983, SAV began its return to the Potomac, a return that included the invasive hydrilla. Boaters and others fear hydrilla's choking behavior and prolific reproductive capacity, while some view any increase in aquatic plant life as a symbol of vastly improving water quality.

Early in the 1980s nearly $1 billion had been spent on the sprawling Blue Plains plant, making it one of the most advanced wastewater treatment plants of its size in the world. Blue Plains is presently releasing cleaner water, virtually free of phosphorus, a nutrient considered particularly detrimental to the Potomac's water quality. The issues of sludge disposal, sediment, chlorine, nutrient loads, and oxygen depletions are all on the active agenda, and corrective measures continue. The public, the states, communities, and federal agencies are determined to finish the job. The Interstate Commission will be there to coordinate and assist in these major efforts.

What does the future look like? Well, I can guarantee that the old notions of drawing a "take map" and systematically buying or condemning private land for a national river or an historic park are simply obsolete. A great deal of the land thought to be essential to fill in the pieces for the C & O Canal National Historical Park may never be acquired simply because it was never needed for the canal in the first place. The Park Service is unable to maintain thousands of acres that, for the most part, could be returned to the citizens who had to give them up.

I am from that unpopular school that believes the great rivers in America belong to everyone: fishermen, birdwatchers, backpackers, bicyclists, and canoeists. The Potomac is one of those rivers. Like the fisherman's widow who scans the sea searching for her lost husband, I continue to watch for the designation of the "Potomac National River," or its equivalent. Meanwhile, I will continue to remind anyone who will listen of the need to love, protect, and care for our Potomac. I'll see you on the river.

Sources

Chapter 1. HARD ROCKS AND SOFT

Abar, Anthony. Director, Bureau of Mines, State of Maryland. Personal communication, October 9, 1992.

Bjerstedt, T. W. 1986. *Regional Stratigraphy and Sedimentology of the Lower Mississippian Rockwell Formation and Purslane Sandstone Based on the New Sideling Hill Road Cut*, pp. 69–94. Maryland Geological Survey, Baltimore, Maryland.

Sideling Hill

Maryland Geological Survey, *Geologic Map of Maryland, 1968*. Covers Allegheny Valley and Ridge, South Mountain anticlinorium and Frederick Valley, western Piedmont, metasedimentary rocks, and Coastal Plain. Can be purchased at the Sideling Hill Exhibit Center located at the Sideling Hill Cut, Maryland, Route 48, west of Hancock, Maryland.

Professional geologists are on duty at the Sideling Hill Exhibit Center to explain details of the cut and its significance.

Chapter 2. RUNNING THE RIVER

Highlights of a personal through-trip from Westernport to tidewater by canoe and thoughts on the trip to the mouth of the Potomac.

Traps

Strandberg, Carl H., and Ray Tomlinson. 1969. Photoarchaeological Analysis of Potomac River Fish Traps. *American Antiquity* 34(3):312–319. Description of photoarchaeological techniques used to survey a section of the Potomac River below Harpers Ferry to the lower end of Heaters Island. Thirty-six stone structures, a navigation weir constructed by the Potomac Company, and a major Indian village site were identified.

Snyder, Joseph J. IV. 1967. The Heater's Island Site, a Preliminary Report. *Journal of the Archaeological Society of Maryland* 3(2):154–161. Baltimore. Historical background of the Piscataway confederacy from A.D. 1500–1700 to the present with particular emphasis on their movement in 1698 to Conoy (Heaters) Island. Massive fish traps at the lower end of Heaters.

Chapter 3. EARLY AWAKENINGS

Browning, Meshach. 1859. *Forty Four Years of the Life of a Hunter.* J. B. Lippincott Company, reprinted by Appalachian Background, Oakland, Maryland. Living and surviving in the Appalachian highlands from Browning's birth in Frederick County in 1781 to his later life in Allegany and Garrett counties where the Potomac and the Youghiogheny rise. Browning's book gives the reader a vivid look at highland country life and what it was like before Browning's death in 1859.

Cook, Carolyn Baucom. 1979. *Journal of the Alleghenies* 15:3–15. Account of the history and geography of the South Branch Valley, and more on the Fairfax Stone.

Everstine, Dr. Carl N. 1985. The Potomac River and Maryland's Boundaries. *Maryland Historical Magazine* 80:4. Maryland Historical Society. The late Dr. Everstine is the author of a number of books and articles on Maryland's legal history. This provides a comprehensive discussion on Maryland's charter boundaries and details the difficulties of early surveyors and woodsmen in locating "the first fountain of the river of Pattowmack" as it was written into the Maryland Charter of 1632. Also discussed is the function of the Fairfax Stone, the Potomac Stone, the Deakins Line, and the north side of the river's bank as a Maryland boundary.

Federal Writers Project, American Guide Series. 1937. *Washington City and Capital,* pp. 30–34. U.S. Government Printing Office, Washington, D.C. Life among the early Nacotchtanks on the Anacostia River to contrasting modern times as Charles Curtis, a Kaw Indian, became Vice-President of the United States.

Gude, Gilbert. 1984. *Where the Potomac Begins: A History of the North Branch Valley.* Seven Locks Press, Cabin John, Maryland.

Gutheim, Frederick. 1949. *The Potomac.* Grosset & Dunlap, New York. Covers the entire Potomac from early development to contemporary times.

Humphrey and Chambers with an Afterword by Stephen R. Potter. 1965. *Ancient Washington American Indian Cultures of the Potomac Valley,* George Washington University Studies No. 6 (2d edition). Coastal Plain cultures left their mark on the future site of the nation's capital.

Kavanagh, Maureen. 1984. Prehistoric Occupation of the Monocacy River Region. In *Piedmont Archeology,* pp. 40–54. Archeological Society of Virginia Special Publication No. 10. Three years of intensive archaeological reconnaissance and testing by the Maryland Geological Survey from 1978 to 1980.

Means, Howard. 1990. The Great Outdoors. *The Washingtonian Magazine,* April, pp. 124–160. Washington, D.C., and environs from the age of the dryptosaurus, a unique member of the dinosaur family to today's crises of deer overpopulation.

Merley, Merritt. 1990. *Traveling the National Road.* Overlook Press, Woodstock, New York. From passage through the primeval wilderness over buffalo traces to today's modern highway. Washington's journey to deliver Virginia Governor's ultimatum to the French. Crosses Allegheny River with Christopher Gist, December 1753, on his return to Cumberland.

Metcalf, Paul. 1982. *Waters of Potomac.* North Point Press, San Francisco. A documentary history of the Potomac River. A collage of primary accounts from early settlers and colonists to the 1960s.

Morrison, Charles. 1970. *The Fairfax Line.* McClain Printing Company, Parsons, West Virginia. Notes on the history and geography of the Fairfax land grant inherited by Thomas, Sixth Lord Fairfax.

Potter, Stephen R. 1984. A New Look at the Accokeek Creek Complex. In *The Prehistoric People of Accokeek Creek,* pp. 36–39. Alice Ferguson Foundation, Accokeek, Maryland. Adaptations in the culture of people living in the Archaic period from 8000 B.C. to late prehistory, ca. A.D. 1600, along Piscataway Creek and Mockley Point.

Pousson, John F. 1983. *Archeological Excavations at the Moore Village Site, C & O Canal National Historical Park, Allegany County, Maryland,* Department of Interior/National Park Service. This report is intended primarily as a description and interpretation of the Moore Village site at Oldtown, Maryland, occupied during the fifteenth century A.D.

Schlosnagle, Stephen, and the Garrett County Bicentennial Committee. 1978. *Garrett County, a History of Maryland's Tableland.* McClain Printing

Company, Parsons, West Virginia. Begins with the first visit by Europeans, the Winslow-Mayo surveying party who, in 1736, were attempting to find the northwestern corner of the Great Northern Neck land tract of Thomas, Virginia's Sixth Lord Fairfax, by order of the King of England.

Place Names

Lowdermilk, Will H. 1971. *History of Cumberland.* Regional Publishing Company, Baltimore, Maryland.

Morrison, Charles. 1971. *Wappatomaka, a Survey of the History and Geography of the South Branch Valley.* McClain Printing Company, Parsons, West Virginia.

Chapter 4. WASHINGTON'S PATOWMACK COMPANY

Manuscripts of the Minnesota Historical Society (1754) 1769–1796, I. *Washington and the Potomac.* These documents form a unit, all dealing with the navigation of the Potomac and James rivers, covering the period 1754–1796. Thirty-eight pieces, including three pen sketches make up the collection. Most documents are copied in George Washington's hand. All papers are endorsed by Washington. Covers existing states of navigation, sluice navigation, lock and dam navigation, types and extent of cargoes, profits and losses, and the peculiarities of operating freight boats on the Potomac River. On file with the Minnesota Historical Society, Minneapolis, edited by Grace L. Nute.

Potomac Company: Report of John Mason, Esq. to the Secretary of the Treasury, January 20, 1808. Excerpts can be found in Corra Bacon-Foster (1911).

Senate Document No. 28, January 27, 1823. Letter from the Governor and Council of Maryland transmitting a report of commissioners appointed by Virginia and Maryland in 1821 to Survey the River Potomac, January 27, 1823, printed by order of the Senate of the United States, Washington. Commissioners were required to examine the affairs of the Potomac Company, including the state of navigation of the river, and its susceptibility for improvement to ascertain whether the company complied with the terms of its charter. The document includes a detailed inspection of the Potomac River from the confluence of the South and North branches to Goose Creek (144 river-miles), which is included in the report as Paper C. This document can be found in its entirety in the Senate Document Records, Capitol Building, Washington, D.C.

Ambler, Charles Henry. 1971. *George Washington and the West.* Russell and Russell, New York.

Bacon-Foster, Corra. 1911. Early Chapters in the Development of the Potomac Route to the West. *Proceedings of the Columbia Historical Society,* vol. 15. An early, but respected work on the formation of the Potomac Company and its operation.

Ecker, Grace Dunlop. 1951. *A Portrait of Old Georgetown.* Dietz Press, Richmond, Virginia. (2d edition.) A portrait of old Georgetown from the early days of the Nacotchank Indians through the years of the Potomac Company and the celebration of the opening of the Chesapeake and Ohio Canal on July 4, 1828.

Hulbert, Archer B. 1905. *Washington and the West.* New York. Excerpts from Washington's journal of 1784.

Kauffman, John M. 1973. *Flow East.* McGraw Hill Book Co., New York.

Loftin, Tee. 1989. *Contest for a Capital.* Tee Loftin Publishers, Washington, D.C. Accounts of Washington's 1784 trip West, the Potomac Company, and the Mount Vernon Compact.

National Geographic—Potomac River and Chesapeake and Ohio Canal
Great Falls of the Potomac, March 1928
Approaching Washington by Tidewater Potomac, March 1930
Washington Through the Years, November 1931
Washington, Home, City and Showplace, June 1937
Roads from Washington, July 1938
Washington, Storehouse of Knowledge, March 1942
Tidewater, Where History Lives, May 1942
Potomac, River of Destiny, July 1945
Down the Potomac by Canoe, August 1948
Waterway to Washington, March 1960
Turnaround Time in West Virginia, June 1976
The Nation's River, Ocotober 1976
The Patowmack Canal, June 1987

Pickell, John. 1856. *A New Chapter in the Early Life of Washington—Narrative History of the Potomac Company.* 2 parts. Burt Franklin, New York. Part 2 begins with Washington's travels to the West after the close of the Revolutionary War in September 1784. It discusses the formation of the Potomac Company and its operation to the transfer of the company's charter to the Chesapeake and Ohio Canal Company in 1828.

Reber, James Q. 1974. *Potomac Portrait.* Liveright, New York. Black and white photographs of the Potomac in its many moods.

Ritter, Halsted L. 1931. *Washington as a Business Man.* Sears Publishing Company, New York. See especially, Chapter 10, Western Navigation, pp. 149–169.

Smith, Osgood R. 1983. *Present Reminders of Early Commerce on the Potomac River above Washington.* National Park Service, Great Falls, Maryland. Dr. Smith, a retired fishery biologist, poles upstream in a canoe as far as the Seneca Breaks to satisfy his interest in evident improvements made in and along the Potomac River in the days of the Potomac Company.

Thomas, James W., and T. J. C. Williams. 1969. *History of Allegany County, Maryland.* Regional Publishing Company, Baltimore. 2 volumes. (Originally published in 1923.) The Potomac Navigation Company, chapter 11, vol. 1, pp. 201–210, provides a good look at early boat commerce on the Potomac and its tributaries and how it was conducted. It also takes a close look at Potomac Company operations from the Savage River to the Georgetown wharves and the kinds and extent of trade that developed. This is one of the few social commentaries available on the daily lives of Potomac river freight boatmen, their crews, and families.

Tilp, Frederick. 1978. *This Was Potomac River.* Self-published, Alexandria, Virginia. The tidal Potomac below Washington. The Potomac from early days of the Indians along the lower shores of the river to Rachel Carson's *Silent Spring.*

Turner, Ella Mae. 1930. *James Rumsey—Pioneer in Steam Navigation.* Mennonite Publishing House, Scottdale, Pennsylvania. Rumsey's role as "Principal Manager" of the Potomac Company and its works at Great Falls is discussed in Chapter 3.

Washington Quarterly Magazine 1 (July 1823). This begins with a timely editorial on internal improvements. From there, the document repeats a portion of *Senate Document No. 28,* but is more legible than the original Senate report. It does not include the day-by-day diary of the inspection trip.

Freshet Riders

Four stalwart canoeists ride a flood event from Oldtown to Hancock to sample an early freshet, similar to those run by the early boatmen. Author's companions: John T. Stanton, Robert L. Farr, and Osgood R. Smith.

Joe Ayers and His Bateau

The 49-foot-long James River flatboat, *Minnie Lee,* weighing in at one ton, was brought up from Columbia, Virginia, Joe Ayers's home ground, astride a trailer frame rigged to take *Minnie* and her crew over 100 miles north to float the Potomac River. *Minnie Lee's* crew included Joe Ayers, Craig Foutz from Fluvanna County, Virginia, Dave Brown of Charlottesville, Virginia, Joe's brother-in-law, Paul Parrish, and Warren O'Brien. The 17-day run from Cumberland to Great Falls was truly a virtuoso performance. The ponderous boat was skillfully guided by *Minnie Lee's* four-man crew and all rapids were run from Cumberland to Great Falls. Citizens in the valley who saw this unique historic re-enactment are still talking about it.

Chapter 5. RACE FOR THE OHIO

Hungerford, Edward. 1918. *The Story of the Baltimore and Ohio Railroad, 1827-1927.* G. P. Putnam's Sons, New York. 2 volumes. Volume 1 covers the early history of both the B & O Railroad and the C & O Canal. Volume 2 continues with principal emphasis on the expansion of the B & O Railroad west of the Alleghenies.

Sanderlin, Walter. 1946. *The Great National Project, a History of the Chesapeake and Ohio Canal.* Johns Hopkins Press, Baltimore. Dr. Sanderlin's history of the canal grew out of a doctoral dissertation at the University of Maryland and draws heavily upon the records of the National Archives. For many years, this 316-page work has been recognized as one of the premier references on the Chesapeake and Ohio Canal.

Stover, John F. 1987. *History of the Baltimore and Ohio Railroad.* Purdue University Press, West Lafayette, Indiana. This amply illustrated volume reviews the history of the B & O Railroad from its uneasy beginnings in Baltimore in 1828 to the installation of a fiber optics communications system in 1983 along what are now CSX rights-of-way.

Chapter 6. CHESAPEAKE AND OHIO CANAL: HEYDAY AND DEMISE

Hahn, Thomas F. 1982. *Towpath Guide to the C & O Canal.* Canal and Transportation Center, Shepherdstown, West Virginia.

Kytle, Elizabeth. 1983. *Home on the Canal.* Seven Locks Press, Cabin John, Maryland. History of the C & O Canal and recollections of eleven men and women who lived and worked on it.

Drawing of the Incline Plane tracks and river surroundings is by Jan Thomas of Rockville, Maryland, from a National Park Service sketch *Outlet Incline, Chesapeake and Ohio Canal 1876–1889.*

Sanderlin, Walter S. 1946. *The Great National Project.* Johns Hopkins Press, Baltimore.

Chapter 7. LIFE ALONG THE RIVER

Charles Mill. My deep appreciation to Mrs. Janet Charles and her daughter, Mrs. Christine Jarvis of Clear Spring, Maryland, for the use of Mrs. Jarvis's story of yesterday's grist mill operations at the family (Charles) mill, which is located along the Potomac River and the C & O Canal.

The Trip of the Rudder Grange. From the diary of the late William Wallace Frantz, father of Mrs. Hilda Cushwa of Clear Spring, Maryland. Mrs. Cushwa is an inspiration to all who value and seek to preserve the cherished events of yesteryear.

Magnolia. Alice Myers of Paw Paw, West Virginia, has an excellent recall of times gone by in Magnolia. Facts were also gathered from conversations with citizens of Paw Paw over an extended period of time.

Thunder in the Mountains, Plunder Underneath. These are real-life scenes developed from years of family discussion with Uncle Junior Laughry of Rowlesburg and Uncle Edgar Fike of Grafton, West Virginia. Extended conversations with George Jennings of Parsons, West Virginia, and recent interviews with Mr. Leon Steyer of Davis, West Virginia, former supervisor for the Davis Coal and Coke Company.

Heaters Island. From extended conversations with Mr. and Mrs. Jesse Miskell at their home in Dargan, Maryland.

The Shawnee Canoe Club. Deepest appreciation to Mr. J. Henry Holzshu, the late Mrs. Eleanor Holzshu, the late Mr. L. Leslie Helmer, Mrs. Helen S. Helmer, and Mr. Howard Buchanan, all of Cumberland, Maryland, for their fond memories of the Shawnees and their unique adventures photographed on the Potomac River and its North and South branches, and to Lee Struble, curator, C & O Canal National Historical Park, for his invaluable assistance.

Y-Camp. Conversations with C. William Gilchrist, James Lemmert, the late Mrs. Eleanor Holzshu, Mr. J. Henry Holzshu, Mrs. Elizabeth Brice Van Keuren, the late Mr. J. Leslie Helmer, and Dr. Tim Lewis.

Chapter 8. A PARK IS BORN

Details of the coming of age of the C & O Canal National Historical Park are derived from a personal knowledge of the canal park, its operation, and history over a period of many years (Superintendent of the C & O Canal Park for 10 years and Advisory Commission Manager for 15 years). There is an excellent source of information covering the details of the Justice William O. Douglas hike, how it was organized and its day-by-day chronology that can be found in the chapter entitled "The C & O Canal Hike," by Jack Durham, in *The Living Wilderness* 19(48):1–26. Spring 1954.

Letter from Assistant Secretary of the Interior transmitting *A Joint Reconnaissance Survey Report Made by the Bureau of Pubic Roads of the Depart-*

ment of Commerce and the National Park Service upon the Advisability and Practicability of Constructing a Parkway along the Route of the Chesapeake Canal between Great Falls and Cumberland, Maryland, Pursuant to Public Law 618. 80th Congress, 2d Session House Document No. 687. GPO, Washington, D.C. 1950.

Chapter 9. THE RIVER RUNNETH OVER

Information on floods and ice jams on the Potomac came from personal knowledge of the details of each flood and their aftermaths from 1936 to present. Floods of 1889 and 1924 and their aftermaths are chronicled in newspaper accounts and personal recollections of Potomac Valley residents. I monitored almost every aspect of the Killer Flood from the upper South and North Branches of the Potomac to tidewater, before, during, and after the event.

Chapter 10. POTOMAC BE DAMMED

Anyone growing up in the Washington area is acquainted with details of and events leading to the fifty years of healing the Potomac. The Corps of Engineers' well-meaning attempts to store water above Washington and cope with the cleansing of the Potomac are also familiar issues to all those living in the Washington area.

Newman, N. Russell. P.E., Jennings Randolf Reservoir Manager. Personal communication, September 27, 1990.

Chapter 11. GUARDIANS OF THE RIVER

Interstate Commission on the Potomac River Basin. 1990. *Healing a River, the Potomac 1940–1990,* The Interstate Commission on the Potomac River Basin, Rockville, Maryland. I presently serve as commissioner for the State of Maryland ICPRB.

Potomac Basin Reporter 47(10), November-December 1991, and 48(1), January 1992.

Chapter 12. CHASING RAINBOWS

The Daily Mail, "Officials Ease Warnings on Upper Potomac Fish," March 25, 1992, Hagerstown, Maryland.

Interviews with George H. Shoemaker, Plant Superintendent, Upper Potomac River Commission, Westernport, Maryland, May 23, 1987 and September 27, 1990.

Interviews with Bob Bachman, Chief, Fresh Water Fisheries, Department of Natural Resources, Maryland, October 9, 1990, and public address, November 2, 1990, Conference on Greenways, Ellicott City, Maryland.

Library Collections

My deep thanks go to John Frye of the Western Maryland Room of the Washington County Free Library for allowing full access to the library's priceless collection of books and papers that relate to historical events in the Potomac Valley and along the C & O Canal and the Potomac River.

A special note of appreciation also goes to the Executive Director of the Interstate Commission on the Potomac River Basin and staff for encouraging full access to their vast and specialized library of water resource material and rare books on related subject matter.

Index

215